GULL IVER'S RAMBLINGS

recorded by

Alick Hartley

Non-government sanity warning

Readers are strongly advised not to take seriously any of the so-called information or dubious ideas contained in this book.

Author's Introduction

Mr. Gull Iver regularly listens to BBC Radio 4/World Service whilst having his breakfast. He then takes his two dogs for a walk in the nearby park. As he keeps his eye on his dogs, he meditates on the snippets of information which he has gleaned from the BBC.

Sometimes, he is joined by another dog walker. In this event, the two jointly 'put the world to rights' in a sensible restrained manner. However, if Gull has to walk on his own, his imagination may really run riot. Sometimes, he is under the delusion that he is a junior minister seeking guidance from his boss, the Chief Minister (C.M.) Sometimes, he is under the delusion that he is a news reporter seeking information from the C.M. On other occasions, he is just imagining. The words "I" and "P.L." (Pack leader) in the text refer to Mr. Gull Iver and not to the author.

The author was simply an amanuensis. No, don't panic, that is not contagious and the author is taking tablets to control it.

The various topics in the book are not in chronological order or any other logical order.

The author disassociates himself completely from the misinformation and wild ideas contained in the book. He only wrote it in the perhaps vain hope that reading the whole book might give rise to at least one smile or chuckle.

It is believed that Mr.Gull Iver emigrated to Outer Bongolia on the day that the final version of the book was sent to the printers.

Contents 1

Contents 2

Page   Topic

Contents 3

Page Topic

The territory of Rockitania

"Good morning, C.M. May I ask you a few questions about Rockitania ?"

"Good morning, John. Yes, I am always happy to help the B.B.C."

"Can you explain why sovereignty is so important now that we are all Europeans ? I thought that the European Union was supposed to do away with these minor squabbles."

"I'm sorry, but I can't answer that. It would be a breach of national security."

"Can you answer questions about the practical details of dual sovereignty ?"

"Certainly. All practical details have been resolved on the principle of absolute parity between the two cultures."

"So, what will be the official language, English or Lickrish?"

"Neither. It will be French."

"And what will be the official currency, the Euro or the Pound?

"Neither. It will be the American dollar."

"Will motorists drive on the left or on the right?"

"Oh, that's an easy one. Straight down the middle."

"And what about bull-fighting? Will that be allowed?"

"Yes, but only on Monday, Wednesday or Friday. Matafighters will only be able to stick lances into the right side of the bull, not into the left side."

"Thank you, C.M. That makes everything absolutely crystal clear. Just one last question - will the residents of Rockitania have any say in the matter?"

"Oh, well, I suppose so."

"Thank you, C.M., I'm glad to hear that. It might just have a bearing on the matter. Of course, it might be considered a human right to be governed by the country that you wish."

"Off the record, John, I cannot understand why they wish to acquire a discontented minority in the South. I would have thought that they had more than enough on their plate with a discontented minority in the North. Don't quote me on that, but you can, of course, leak it in the usual way 'from a reliable source'.

Voter apathy or just frustration ?

Two people decided to celebrate by having an evening meal out in a small rural town. In the town, there were just three places to eat - The Bluebell Bistro, The Red Rose Restaurant and the Orange-Blossom 'Otel. Each of these offered its own set manifesto, sorry, I mean MENU (Table d'Hôte).

The two people first tried the Bluebell Bistro. They asked for Oxtail soup ; Chicken, Roast Potatoes & Peas ; Fruit salad. The waiter said "I'm sorry, sir. We can serve you the Fruit Salad, but with it you must have Tomato soup, then Roast Beef, Jacket potatoes and Sprouts.

Then they tried the Red Rose Restaurant. Again they asked for Oxtail soup ; Chicken, Roast Potatoes & Peas ; Fruit salad. The waitress said "I'm sorry, Sir. We can serve you the Oxtail Soup, but with it you must have Roast Beef, Jacket potatoes and sprouts, then Jam Sponge pudding.

Finally, they tried the Orange-blossom 'Otel. Once again, they asked for Oxtail soup ; Chicken, Roast Potatoes & Peas ; Fruit salad. Here, the waitress said "I'm sorry, Sir. We can serve you the Chicken Roast potatoes and Peas, but with it you must have Tomato soup and then Jam Sponge pudding.

The two people then said to each other "Oh, let's forget it. We'll go home and watch television."

Was that 'apathy' or 'frustration' ? The same thing applies to elections. Of course, at one time, voting was simple. The Conservative Party represented the aristocracy, the land owners, the bosses, privatisation. The Labour Party represented the workers and the unemployed. The Liberal Party was somewhere in between. People knew exactly for whom to vote.

Now the Conservative Party is roughly the same as before. New Labour is, well, New Labour. I am glad that they did not choose a **White** Rose. The Liberal Democrats are left to represent people who are 'left of centre', but many electors just feel completely confused and baffled, if not betrayed.

Rumour of transfer

Is there any truth in the rumour that Buttercup Comprehensive are paying Sunflower High School seven million pounds transfer fee for their Head of Mathematics ?

Carbon dioxide emission

"Excuse me, Chief, but isn't it time that we did something towards the Carbon dioxide emission target set for us by Monsieur B Russels ?"

"Don't worry, Dafydd, it's all under control. By opening up parcel delivery to free competition, instead of just one Royal Mail van driving round the country, we now have five or six parcel delivery vans racing round the country. I seem to see a new logo everyday. That should help towards our carbon dioxide target. If that doesn't do the trick, we'll soon be opening up the letter delivery service to private competition as well, so that should help."

Countryside paths

"Good morning, C.M. This morning, I heard two reports on Radio 4. The first said that most farmers' incomes have decreased drastically, in fact, some have become negative. They desperately need some additional income. The second said that ramblers and other users of country paths are complaining because country paths are not maintained properly and gates and stiles are in disrepair. Some paths are even deliberately obstructed by the farmers concerned. Can't we do something about it?"

"Thank you, Helen, but that's got nothing to do with us. We're only governing the country, we don't run it."

The introduction of the metric system

Circa 1965 Henceforth all school examinations will be taken iyyyyyyyyn metric units and not 'Imperial measures'. Every school in the country spent thousands of pounds replacing their 'Imperial measure' textbooks by metric textbooks, destroying the old textbooks.

For 30 years, employers complained about the standard of education because youngsters did not even know how many pounds there were in a stone or feet in a yard.

Circa 2001 A shopkeeper was fined for using pounds weight to sell vegetables.

....

"Bonjour, pardon, I mean good morning. I would like to buy some of that material. Do you sell it in yards or in metres?"

"Oh, metres. I could be severely fined now, if I sold it to you in yards. Yards and miles were in Imperial Measure. The only people who are still using Imperial Measure are the Americans. Of course, they left the Empire in 1776."

....

"Excuse me, monsieur policeman. Does that sign there with the 30 in a circle really mean that I have to keep below 30 kilometres an hour?"

"Oh, no, sir. It means below 30 miles per hour."

⟨⟨ Brigitte, ces Anglais sont imbéciles. ⟩⟩

Social Justice

"Excuse me, C.M., but when is the Party going to do something about its long standing commitment to the redistribution of wealth from the richest to the poorest ?"

"Don't worry, Amina. It's all under control. Every week, the national lottery is producing several millionaires - sometimes the winners get 3 millions or even up to 14 millions. There are television quiz shows doing the same sort of thing. It's possible for some one with a good memory to 'earn' half a million or a million in one evening. I believe that I heard one winning teacher say that he had won more money that evening that he could earn in three months for his normal work."

"But, C.M., isn't all that taking money from poorer people and making more very rich people ? Isn't the redistribution of wealth going the wrong way ?"

"When the party started, did they say in which direction the redistribution of wealth had to go ?"

"But, C.M., what about the Protestant Work Ethic which was one of the foundations on which Socialism was built?"

"I'm sorry, Amina, but I've absolutely no idea what you're talking about. I've never heard of either the Protestant Work Ethic or Socialism. They sound to me a bit like the weird ideas that Old Labour had. We abandoned those some time ago. You really must get up to speed. Mind you, with your public-spirited and altruistic ideas, I really wonder whether you wouldn't be more at home in another party."

Environmental break (1)

Please excuse me for a minute. I have to clean up after my two dogs. They can't reach the 'dog litter bins'.

This morning's snippet

A government committee reported that 10% of operating theatre time was being wasted due to staff shortages, particularly the surgeon taking annual leave at very short notice. They said that, if hospitals adopted 'best practice', they could achieve the target of 90% usage of operating theatre time. I actually heard the snippet twice, so I am sure that I **aud it** correctly,

We've got a mandate !

I don't know why, but this saying always reminds me of a very famous tipster Prince something or other who used to attend a racecourse shouting "I've got a horse". I have often wondered whether the Prince gave the names of different horses to different people in order to ensure that he always had some satisfied customers. Sorry, back to the mandate.

Whatever the C.M. decides to do, he always covers himself with "We've got a mandate." presumably referring to the last party manifesto. However, the only mandate which the majority of the electors in a particular constituency has given, the only thing indicated by a **X**, is for a certain person to represent them in the House of Commons.

It might be said that the certain person is the member of a certain political party so that the vote is a vote for that party with its particular manifesto. This is not necessarily true. There have been several instances of members 'crossing the floor of the House' to join another party. Those members do not ask the permission of the voters who elected them. They just decide and do it.

I believe that the correct action for the 'honourable member' to take would be to resign and then stand as a candidate for his/her new party at the consequent by-election. Of course, that is supposing that his/her new party would adopt him/her as their candidate. I don't think that there is a law against obtaining a vote by false pretences, but I have heard a rumour that one group of electors were drafting a class action to sue for compensation for being deprived of parliamentary representation. Come to think of it, if the Judge awarded a token sum of one pound to everyone who voted for the candidate, it would amount to a tidy sum!

Of course, this mandate does not work the other way round. A government may have a mandate to do something but that does not mean that it does it. For example, a government might have a mandate to ban fox-hunting with dogs, but ....

Joined-up government

A splendid idea. Pity that the Inland Revenue cannot agree with Customs and Excise about when the financial year begins and ends. Perhaps the 6th April was Henry VIII's birthday, so we can't possibly change that. Of course, most businesses now do their accounts on computers and, to the best of my knowledge, all computer accounts programs work in proper calendar months.

Big businesses no doubt have a VAT section and a PAYROLL section operating independently. However, small businesses just have one accounts section which deals with both. It is unnecessarily confusing that a wage paid on the 3rd April comes in 2001-2002 for PAYE purposes but in 2002-2003 for the company's year-end accounts.

If we can put a man onto the moon, it shouldn't be beyond the wit of man or woman to bring the two years into line.

....

"Excuse me, C.M. If and when we adopt the Euro, on what date will that happen, the 1st April or the 6th April?"

"That will have to be agreed with the European Central Bank. I should imagine that it might be 14th July."

P.A.Y.E. and National Insurance

"Excuse me, C.M., but the proprietor of a small business has come up with an idea for simplifying the laborious work that such employers have in calculating PAYE and employERS contribution to national insurance and employEES contribution to national insurance. He suggests that these three should be amalgamated into one payment."

"He gave an example

Present arrangement

Wage	£30	Cost to employer	£34
PAYE	£ 5	Treasury receives	£12
EmployERS NI	£ 4	Employee receives	£22
EmployEES NI	£ 3		

Proposed arrangement

Gross Wage	£34	Cost to employer	£34
Deduction	£12	Treasury receives	£12
		Employee receives	£22 "

Of course, all the other things - Sick Pay, Maternity Pay, Tax credits etc - which we have contrived to inflict on the poor defenceless employers will have to be considered. It's amazing what you can get away with if you remember Softly, softly, lumber employer."

"Thank you, Helen, but I thought the countryside was your responsibility?"

"Yes, C.M., but that was last week. This week, I'm part of the Treasury."

"Oh, very well, then. Helen, do you realise how many people would be put out of work if we simplified the system?"

"Yes, C.M., but if they are intelligent enough to cope with all the intricacies of PAYE and NI etc etc etc, they could be retrained for something useful like nursing, teaching or simply taking blood samples from farm animals for testing in a laboratory."

"But how do we change from the present arrangement to the proposed arrangement?"

"Simple. All we have to do is to issue a directive to the effect that on some convenient date

(a)   all existing wages are henceforth increased by the exact amount of the employer's contribution to NI

(b)   the employer will henceforth deduct from the Gross Wages and pay to the treasury one payment comprising the existing PAYE, employer's contribution and the employee's contribution

For future years, there would be one table specifying one deduction."

Environmental break (2)

"Wait a minute, boss.   We've got to clear up after a lot of human beings."

"Rover, you're a retriever so you've got a soft, gentle mouth. You clear up the glass bottles while I take care of the plastic bottles and cans. Be very careful with the broken glass, it could be dangerous. Put them in that rubbish bin - it's only a yard or two away. I cannot understand why humans think that such a beautiful park looks more attractive when decorated with every imaginable kind of litter. But then I'm only a dog with no aesthetic sense."

What do people really want?

I haven't got the luxury of being able to commission a survey, I can only rely on conversations with many people in different situations. My impression is that most people want **basic services** - usually monopolies - to be either national, county or municipal.

Basic services include the NHS, state education, everything requiring networks (the telephone system, the railway network, the water supply, the gas supply), air traffic control, police, social services. Other enterprises - businesses - which are not basically monopolies can be open to free market competition.

What were we given ?

Well, the 1945 government started off very well. They nationalised all the basic services, but later they got carried away and nationalised almost everything in sight. Fortunately for me, they did not get round to my rusty old bike.

Then the next lot spent time and money privatising much that had been nationalised, except that the railway network, which pre-war had been just four regional companies, was divided into I don't know how many different companies. Ask the general public what they think about our railways.

And we are still pressing on with the idea that 'public' must be inefficient and bad whereas 'private' must be efficient and good. Surely the ethic behind a 'service' is quite different from the ethic behind a 'business'. The first should aim to maximise the service provided to the public, the second aims to maximise the profits and the dividends paid to the shareholders. If state or municipal services do not produce the best results, then the fault lies with the man or woman at the top and the philosophy of the workers.

Celebration?

"Excuse me, C.M., but, after the meeting this morning, I overheard some of our backbenchers muttering something about a booze-up in a brewery. Are we having a celebration? What have we got to celebrate?"

'Share-a-dog'

"Excuse me, P.L.. Could we talk for a minute? Fido and I have been thinking. We know that we are both very lucky to be living with you. We are very rarely left on our own to guard the house and we can keep each other company. But we meet lots of dogs who live alone, apart from humans. Often both grown-ups in the household are out at work and the children are at school, so they are left alone in their house, sometimes for hours on end. Some of them are let out for a while at lunchtime and some of them can look out of a window to relieve their boredom, but by no means all of them. Some of them get into trouble for damaging the furnishings - they are not really naughty but they just get so bored.

At the same time, we know of lots of retired people, most of them living alone and perhaps not fit enough to go out. Rover and I thought that it would be a good idea if, instead of leaving their dog alone in the house, people could 'park' their dog for working hours with a lonely retired person. It would be very welcome company and entertainment for the retired person and be much more fun for the dog. Of course, the retired person need have no responsibility for either food or exercise for the dog.

We've mentioned it to a lot of our four-legged friends and they think it's a great idea. Pack Leader, could you possibly mention it to all your dog-owning friends?"

Communicating with Whitehall

This morning, during an interview, the interviewee said that she had written to a Government department and RECEIVED A REPLY. We hear so many people say that they have written to one Government department or another, but not received a reply, that to hear that someone had received a reply came as a bit of a shock. Mind you, it might have made a difference that the interviewee who received the reply was Her Majesty the Queen! (Beg pardon, Your Majesty, no disrespect intended. PLEASE don't send me to the Tower. I'm not supposed to eat beef.)

The Government is well supplied with Public Relations spin doctors who are skilled in brainwashing us with what we ought to want or need, also what the Government is going to give us. Usually these two seem to bear a striking resemblance to each other.

On the other hand, there doesn't seem to be a central P.R. department equipped to RECEIVE letters containing ideas or suggestions from the general public, sending a postcard to the sender to acknowledge the receipt of the letter, forwarding the contents of the letter to the appropriate department and then **ensuring** that the writer of the letter receives a relevant and considered reply.

Of course, as we only elect governments who are both omniscient and infallible, there is really no need for them to receive any ideas or suggestions. But it might be worthwhile just to humour us and keep us happy, in the delusion that what we think actually matters.

Perhaps the Government should also have a 24 hour team listening to the BBC Radio 4/World Service, particularly Farming Today, and passing on the information gleaned to the appropriate departments. I have great respect for the interviews and discussions on the BBC - they are very balanced and informative.

Of course, the extra Public Relations staff needed must not increase the size of the civil service. They could be either Agency number 2457, Trust number 578 or Quango number 256.

Proportional representation

"Excuse me, C.M., but I'm a little worried about the Hawkvale by-election which isn't far away. The latest opinion poll shows that the far right Grammatical party stand a good chance of winning. The results of the poll gave Conservative 20%, Grammatical 30%, Lib Dem 22% and New Labour 28%. It would be dreadful if the Grammatical party got in. We would have to start saying 'Try to do something' instead of 'Try and do something', 'procrastination' instead of 'prevarication' when we mean 'delay doing something', talk about 'railway stations' instead of 'train stations' and 'moving quickly' instead of 'moving fast'. We wouldn't be able to use a preposition to end a sentence **with** and we wouldn't be able to **legally** split an infinitive, whatever one is. We would have to learn spelling, grammar and punctuation. It just doesn't bear thinking about."

"On the 'first past the post system', the Grammaticals will be elected. I know that it only affects about 90 thousand people, but it sets a precedent for the whole country. I wonder if we shouldn't have adopted proportional representation by a single transferable vote as recommended by the Lib Dems."

"I don't see what George has got to do with it, Rosemary. P.R. is a useful ploy to keep the Lib Dems on our side when things are a bit dodgy, but I wouldn't even contemplate it when we've got an overwhelming majority."

"But C.M., in the old days when the Conservatives were on the right, the Lib Dems in the centre and Labour on the left, P.R. would have elected the Lib Dems. But now with the Conservatives on the right, ourselves New Labour and the Lib Dems on the left, if the Conservative candidate was eliminated, all those votes would come to us. We're as safe as houses."

"Perhaps you're right, Rosemary, but there is always tactical voting. If all the conservatives vote New Labour and all the New Labour people vote conservative, everything will turn out all right. Anyway, cobber, if the Grammaticals did get in, they would have an uphill fight now that all our TV channels have been sold to an antipodean millionaire, true dinkum they would. Bye now!"

Road Tax, Petrol and Insurance

"Excuse me, C.M., but Mr.Khan, one of the men in my department, has come up with a new idea. You know that we are worried about youngsters particularly driving without a driving licence, road tax or insurance. In the event of an accident - which is only too likely - this can have drastic consequences for an innocent party involved in the accident, that is if they are still living."

"Also, some campaigners representing the older people in society think it is unfair that such people have to pay the same road tax as workers who use their cars very much more. The oldies probably only use their cars for visits to the doctor, dentist or optician and, of course, weekly shopping, perhaps clocking up 5000 miles a year. The workers often clock up 50 000 miles a year."

"Mr. Khan suggests that motor insurance is taken over by the State, that there should be an extra charge per litre on petrol and diesel to pay for the state insurance and another to replace road tax. Of course, there might have to be special arrangements for foreign-owned vehicles."

"It's a brilliant idea, Desmond, but I'm afraid that it's out of the question. We couldn't possibly take over the motor insurance, we're not a socialist government. The road tax idea might be all right, but we would have to get permission from the oil companies, the European Union and the Global Trading Association. Perhaps we could modify the scheme so that we used all the many existing insurance companies with all the oil companies acting as intermediaries. That would make it cumbersome enough to be accepted."

Saving for retirement

"Good morning, C.M. The insurance companies are very worried that people are not saving enough for retirement. They think that we ought to encourage them to pay more into a pension scheme."

"Well, we've made a good step forward, Alison. We've changed the taxation rules slightly so that insurance companies can no longer recover the tax paid on the dividends which they receive on behalf of their customers. This means that to get the same level of pension, people have to pay higher premiums, so we ARE encouraging people to pay more into a pension scheme."

"But, C.M., I thought that the idea was for people to receive bigger pensions so that there would be less need for help from the state."

"Oh well, Alison, they'll just have pay even more."

....

"Hello, Charlie, how's ta bin?"

"Fair to middling, Bert."

"Charlie, if you don't mind me asking, how much a month are you putting aside for use when you retire?"

"Nay, lad, don't be sa daft. Nowt. I know so many people who have worked hard all their lives, grabbing as much overtime as they could get and living frugally, then they've finished up worse off than the people who have taken it easy and squandered all their money. So many of the benefits are means tested that it just doesn't pay to save. People won't be inclined to save seriously until all benefits are universal."

"I see where you are coming from, Charlie, but wouldn't that mean giving money to people who don't really need it?"

"Yes, Bert, but if all benefits were subject to the tax system, you could easily clobber those REALLY rich people through taxation."

National Leaders

Are people trained in the right way to govern the country? In some professions, the experts have either been endowed with or trained in 'the gift of the gab'. That is what enables them to secure such positions. They are trained to 'fight their corner', right or wrong, guilty or not guilty. But are 'the gift of the gab' or rapier-like repartee in the Commons, the sort of qualities needed to make the right decisions in the interest of the public, from whichever part of the House the idea or proposal comes. The qualities really needed in a national leader are logic, imagination, a sense of justice and foresight to anticipate the consequences of each action.

Most people reckon that it takes a newly appointed Head of Department in a secondary school at least twelve months, a whole school year, to get his/her 'feet under the table' before making any substantial changes. The Head of Maths never changes place with the Head of English. But we see Cabinet Ministers moved from one post to another after much shorter periods of time.

Television licences

At a recent gathering of senior citizens, I heard one dear old lady say "It's great that we don't have to pay for a licence to own a television set. Pity that I can't afford some spectacles so that I could watch the programmes. I thought that, in 1945, we were promised that spectacles would be free."

Personally, I wonder why we have television licences. Television and radio are the only services I know in which the cost of production is not affected by the number of consumers using the service or for how many hours they use it. A great deal of both person-hours and money is really completely wasted receiving money for licences, keeping a record of it and sending out detector vans to track down those without a licence. All that waste would be eliminated if we just abandoned licences and paid the cost of the BBC out of general taxation. How little effect would it have on the rates of income tax? Abolishing TV licences would be quite a help to the poorest households and the extra tax would make little difference to the better-off households.

The Upper House

Now that it is generally recognised that the House which is elected is the more important, should it still be called the Upper House which implies superiority. I believe that abolition of the House of Lords has been Labour Party policy since 1911, yes 1911. It is surprising that, at the time of writing, there are no firm proposals regarding the replacement of the House of Lords. This project still seems to be 'on the back burner'.

Although it seems to work - after a fashion - in the U.S.A., I do not recommend a second chamber elected on a regional basis. My suggestions are :
(a) a chamber elected from all the leading professions : a doctor, an engineer, chemist, mathematician, statistician, biologist, teacher, agricultural scientist, a lawyer, etc etc - perhaps a retired but still competent person. In that way, for every debate, there would be at least one person who really knew what he/she was talking about.
(b) a chamber elected on an age basis, so that there would be one or more elected members to represent 18 year old, 19 year old,.............perhaps over 80. This would not be a carbon copy of the other elected chamber and the ever increasing number of older people would feel that their views were being taken into consideration.
(c) a chamber elected by the various religions and denominations, so that there would be one or more members representing Church of England, Roman Catholic, Hindu, Muslim, Sikh, Methodist, Baptist, Humanist, Atheist .... Again, this would not be a carbon copy of the other elected chamber and all sections of the population would feel that their views were being considered..

Electricity, Gas and Water

I do not wish to provoke an argument, but would somebody please explain to me in three letter words why it is more efficient and cheaper to have a third party involved between the producer and the customer. It must cost money - a waste of money - to have financial transactions producer→distributor and distributor→consumer instead of just producer→consumer ... and sometimes the network owner is a different company still.

When both gas and electricity were nationalised, I thought that it was stupid that the two meters were read by two different people instead of just one person. Instead of privatising all three services, why weren't they just combined under national ownership.

Of course, this multiple privatisation does create more employment. Apart from the extra accounting, we need people to persuade us to change from Genpower to Powerman, from Powerman to Gasbrit, from Gasbrit to Genutil and from Genutil to Genpower. All that does not include the time and phone calls that the consumer has to expend trying to persuade the old supplier to cough up any money owing to him/her arising from overpayment before he switched suppliers.

I guess that I'm just not 'with it', so I do wish that someone would help me. If the original organisations could be less efficient than the present set up, their managers should have been shown a 'red card'.

The Mail Service

"Good morning, C.M. I am a little worried about the Post Office or whatever it is called now."

"Good morning, Dafydd. You seem to have an obsession about the Mail service. Whatever is your problem now?"

"Well, C.M., I believe that the Post Office is facing difficulties. With the increasing use of fax machines, they lost a lot of business traffic, particularly to destinations overseas. Now, with the rapidly increasing use of the internet and e-mail, they are losing even more traffic. With e-mail, it is possible to send quite long messages by means of what they call 'enclosures'."

"Oh, you mean the things in which they keep sheep."

"No, C.M., they are not quite that. If it is to remain viable, the Post Office needs more mechanisation and computerisation, but it needs to sustain its present volume of traffic to pay for all that. It needs competition like a hole in the head."

"Nonsense, Dafydd. I am sure that some healthy competition will solve the problem. The competitors will take over all the most remunerative city traffic and all the Post Office will have to worry about is the small amount of traffic to the more distant destinations, like Rural Wales. Then all their problems will have been solved."

Rolling elections

"Good morning, C.M. I am sure that this will make you smile. Some nutcase says that under the present system of electing all the members of parliament at one go, the government may change rapidly from one extreme to the other like the pendulum of a clock. The rapid change can happen literally overnight."

"Well, Sharmila, what does he want in its place?"

"He says that, in many organisations, a third of the committee is replaced each year. Members are elected for a term of three years. This means that there is a certain level of continuity, with no extreme changes from one policy to another. There are always many people on the committee with experience of recent events and the mistakes that have been made. Any major changes in basic policy take place gradually and not suddenly.

"Ha! Ha! Ha! Ha! Ha! Sharmila, you've made my day. Remind me to promote you in the next reshuffle."

School Sports

"C.M., I'm glad to see that you are going to encourage school sports again."

"Yes, Tommy, the problem of childhood obesity is becoming very serious. When all teaching is done by computer, the pupils won't even have the exercise of raising their hands to answer a question."

"C.M., it's a pity that so many schools had to sell off their playing fields because they were short of money. Also so many teachers lost interest in out-of-school activities when one Government minister told the public that teachers only work a six hour day!"

"Nevertheless, Tommy, it's a good idea. We will just have to set schools a target and leave it to each Head to wave his/her magic wand."

Moonlighting

"Good morning, C.M. It is well known that quite a few M.P.s are also members of the Welsh Assembly or the Scottish Parliament. Does this mean that being a member of Parliament is just a part-time job? When I was a teacher, before I became a reporter, I would have found it absolutely impossible to hold down a job in London and simultaneously one in Cardiff or Edinburgh. I appreciate that some members supplement their meagre pay by several directorships, but two government jobs, paid by the taxpayer, seems to be a little different. Perhaps this partly accounts for the majority of empty seats that we see when we watch parliament on television."

Salary awards

"Good morning, Minister. Some time ago, the teachers were awarded an increase in pay, but Heads were told that the total expenditure on salaries had to remain the same. That meant that teachers either had to teach more lessons per week or teach bigger classes. Now that we have awarded ourselves a substantial pay increase, will you be reducing the number of members and constituencies so that members will have to take care of more constituents?

"Don't be silly, Cedric. There is no similarity between ourselves and teachers. We're important. In any case, we have to set an example to all the other spending departments on how to control their expenditure."

Immigrants

From what I hear, our railways are the worst in Europe, we are sending NHS patients to France for treatment, we are importing doctors from Spain and nurses from the West Indies, we work longer hours than the rest of Europe, our prices are higher than they are in the rest of Europe. Would someone please explain to me why so many immigrants are trying to get into the UK instead of staying in France or somewhere else in Euroland?

The only possible explanation that I can see is that we don't have identity cards, but perhaps I'm wrong, as usual.

"We don't even talk the same language."

When we say "We don't even talk the same language", we don't mean that literally. It is just a figure of speech, like saying "He wouldn't recognise a giraffe if he bumped into one." What we really mean is that our views are 'poles apart', immeasurably different. We might say "It may be Mathematics to you but it's all Greek to me." We use these sayings because we realise that, if people don't talk the same language, it is very difficult for them to communicate, let alone become friends.

I am definitely NOT a racist. When I was a teacher, I really enjoyed teaching pupils of different colours and cultural backgrounds. The variety made life much more interesting. Closer to home, it's great to hear someone in a call centre speaking in a Scots accent or a Welsh, almost singing, voice as a change from the usual English accent.

I have a Collie and a Retriever, but I would hate it if dogs were all Retrievers or all Collies - the variety of breeds and temperaments makes dogs much more interesting and fun. Even more so with human beings.

I think that it is the duty of all people of goodwill - I am not going to mention any particular religion - to say 'Good morning' or 'Hello' and smile at people of a different colour when they pass them, just to reassure them that they are welcomed by some people.

But I believe that all inhabitants of this country should be encouraged to learn English, not least for their safety and everyone else's, so that they know what 'Danger' and 'High voltage' etc mean. Much prejudice stems from the fact that some immigrants 'don't speak the same language' that we do.

All immigrants, who are not already fluent in English, should have a 'crash course' - at public expense - before they embark on anything else. That would be a tremendous help to immigrants of school age before they start mainstream school. I do not think that it is at all helpful for children whose mother tongue is not English to be taught in their own language. They MUST be given special help when they first arrive, but then, when they have learned English, they will be able to stand on their own feet.

I am not just advocating English because it is the common language of the United Kingdom, but because it is the common language of **the world**.

Immigrants could be encouraged to maintain their own language for cultural reasons. Many Welsh people are bilingual and most people on the continent speak many languages.

If immigrants are to be housed in 'asylum centres' for six months or so, that would be a splendid opportunity for them to be given a free course in English. If they are already fluent in English, perhaps a free course in computing or some other useful skill. If they were repatriated, at least they would return home grateful to us instead of being resentful.

Family values

"Excuse me, C.M. There's a Mr. Proper Gander here to see you."

"Hello, Proper. How can I help you this morning?"

"Well, C.M. A number of our back-benchers and several religious organisations would like us to make more use of television to promote so-called family values."

"Forget the back-benchers, Proper, they just have to do what they're told. However, I think we ought to try to keep the religious organisations on our side. There must not be any obvious brain-washing and we must maintain the right to free speech. The odd 5% of the population who don't support us must be allowed to say what they think. Of course, we needn't take any notice of what they think."

"We could set targets for the television companies and promise them a tax break if they meet the targets. If we push the same theme over and over again, the public will think that such behaviour is the norm, that it is what is expected of them. I am sure that most people will respond. You know that the only thing in which we are leading Europe, top of the league, is teenage pregnancy. We must not let that honour slip away from us."

"What about saying that, in any program, 60% of the time should be devoted to a married man sleeping with another man's wife, 30% to discussion about the identity of the father of a new baby and 10% to a married woman having an illicit affair with a Catholic Priest. That may sound very ambitious, but I believe that most of the television companies are a long way down that road already."

"Fine, C.M., but you haven't allowed any time for the main story line."

"Oh, yes, well, we'll add 20% for that."

"But that would give us more than 100%."

"Oh, does it, Proper? I forgot to bring my calculator."

"Yes, it would give 120%, which would make it impossible for the television companies to reach all those targets."

"Excellent. You should know by now, Proper, that we only set targets that are impossible to reach, otherwise there would be no one to blame if the results don't satisfy the public. In any event, we would never be able to persuade the Guardian of the Exchequer to give them a tax break."

"Do those targets apply to the medical dramas and the animal rescue dramas?"

"Absolutely, they offer the best opportunities for our message. Oh, when you are talking to the television companies, remind them that, whether it's burglary, blackmail, credit card fraud, smuggling illegal immigrants or whatever, the culprits must get away with it. They must not be either exposed or punished. If they were, many of the viewers might feel repressed. We don't know how much psychological damage that would cause. The companies must encourage selfishness, getting as much as you can for as little as possible. There mustn't be any of this nonsense about job satisfaction or working for the public good."

(Soapiography : "Ennervale", "Corporation Street", "Genpracs", "Holly Town")

Justice? Not proven

"Excuse me, C.M., Alistair MacTavish would like to see you."

"Thank you. Please let him in."

"Hello, Alistair. I believe that you want to discuss the legal system."

"Yes, C.M. Many of my constituents are very worried about the growing number of alleged offenders who are 'getting off on a technicality'. They are unhappy that the only verdicts open to a jury are 'Guilty' and 'Not guilty". Very often, we hear scientists say that "Further research is required" or "There is no evidence either way". Scientists, who can both study statistics which are indisputable and also carry out their own experiments, are often unable to give a definite answer, 'Yes' or 'No'. So why should we expect juries, relying on evidence, sometimes months old, which may or may not be reliable, to give a definite answer 'Guilty' or 'Not guilty'."

"Why don't England and Wales adopt the Scottish system in which 'Not proven' is an acceptable verdict? The verdict 'not proven' has been in existence in Scotland as long as I can remember. The Scots are a canny race. If the use of 'Not proven' was not helpful, I am sure that they would have got rid of it years ago."

"You wouldn't be biased, would you, Alistair?"

"No, C.M., I dinna think so. Ye ken me better than that. Another point to be considered, C.M., is whether the so-called adversarial system is really the best system. Almost everyone has had experience of the effect on the verdict of representation by a good lawyer or a bad lawyer. Shouldn't everyone involved in the process be trying to establish the TRUTH instead of just scoring points off the other side in the hope of WINNING the case?"

"That sounds to me like another foreign idea. Perhaps I'm wrong, but I seem to connect it with Napoleon. Well, Alistair, I will consider those points, but you know that English people are very reluctant to learn anything from anyone else."

Smoking

"Good morning, C.M. I am very worried that we are not making much progress in discouraging smoking. Smoking does save us a lot of money in old age pensions, but it costs us very much more in NHS care than we save in that direction. The problem is particularly acute with young girls."

"I agree, Gwyneth, but we have banned the advertising of cigarettes - except for the special case of motor racing. What more can we do?"

"Well, I think that it is of little value to ban advertising on television when many of the leading female characters in the 'soaps' are puffing away to their heart's content - and peril! Could we, without introducing open censorship, somehow discourage smoking in all 'soaps'? Of course, we would still see smoking in old films, but eventually people would be saying "That must be an old film. Marilyn is smoking." "

"Very well, Gwyneth, see what the television companies say. I suppose they are not owned by the big tobacco companies, are they?"

Reminiscences of World War II

We see many films depicting how the Americans won the war with a little help from the Brits - not forgetting the Dominions, Free Poles, Free French, Free Norwegians and so on. We see very few films depicting the heroism of the fight put up by the Russians and the Chinese. The latter were fighting against the Japanese for years before we were. Perhaps a few such films, available in both Russian and English or Chinese and English, would help to build bridges and friendship with the countries who, within living memory, were our former gallant and invaluable allies.

Reorganising hospitals

"Good Morning, Wendy. I've got some ideas for reorganising our hospitals."

"But, C.M., considering the amount of finance and support that we don't give them, I thought that our hospitals were doing remarkably well. Most of my friends won't have a word said against them."

"That's exactly why we've got to reorganise them - on the same lines as the railways."

"But, C.M. I thought that their lines were too busy already. Oh, sorry, now I see what you mean, but how exactly would it work?"

"We will privatise all the departments, spread amongst many different companies. The Maternity Department would be operated - no, 'run' might be a better word - by Synthetic Baby Foods Ltd, the Geriatric Department and the Intensive Care Department by Lifelong Annuities PLC, the Orthopaedic Department by Artificial Limb Producers, the Oncology Department by Deathwish Tobacco Inc, the Cardiac Department by Olympic Pacemaker Producers and the Haematological Department by the Vampires Society. Also Anaesthetics will be handled by a subsidiary of Gasbrit as an optional extra, chargeable, of course. That should save the NHS quite a lot of money."

"Very good, C.M.. I'll set it in train immediately and make sure that everyone is on the right track."

Capitalism or Socialism

Some people have suggested that it wouldn't matter whether we adopted Capitalism or Socialism if everybody was public-spirited, working for the common good, getting 'job satisfaction' from doing a good job and contributing as much as possible to the community. It wouldn't matter if some aristocrat did inherit half of Mayfair, if he/she used his/her half of Mayfair for the benefit of the general public.

On the other hand, Socialism is no good if it is led by a dictator who sets an example by having gold-plated bath taps and a second palace in the countryside. That is why Mahatma Gandhi gained so much respect. It isn't the political system that matters, it is the attitude of the people.

Striving for 'job satisfaction' has been replaced by striving for money, in other words GREED. The more that people have, the greedier they seem to become. Job satisfaction and greed are subject to the 'trickle down' effect. One or the other starts at the top and trickles down to the bottom. The greatest form of job satisfaction is helping or serving other people.

The strong pound

I'm sorry that I am so ignorant. I was born that way and I become more ignorant every year. This morning, for the 3275th time, I heard somebody blaming the strong pound for all their problems. It was also implied that all the problems would disappear if we abandoned pounds and adopted Euros.

Could someone please explain to me, in very simple English, why the strong pound means that we cannot sell our goods and services? Is a stick any longer if it is measured in feet then when it is measured in metres? Yes, the number of feet will be more than the number of metres, but the actual length will be the same. Is the capacity of the petrol tank of my car any greater if I fill it with so many gallons than if I fill it with so many litres?

Surely the real reason why we cannot sell our goods and services is that our prices are too high, in whatever currency they are expressed. If the pound is strong, too high, then we have to sell things for less pounds. If our prices are too high, it must be because the natural resources we have are not as favourable as those elsewhere **or** our systems are not as efficient as those elsewhere **or** our wages and salaries are too high, perhaps especially those of the so called 'fat cats'.

Please remember that if the government insists that the value of the pound goes down, so will the value of my hard earned pension. Have pity on me!

I am not suggesting that there are no advantages in adopting the Euro. Obviously, it would be helpful when we are on holiday and for business transactions. On the other hand, we would lose control of our base interest rate, the subject of a Bank of England meeting every month, I believe. Control of the interest rate was passed to the Bank of England so that it would be independent of the prevailing Government. If we adopted the Euro, that control would pass to the European Bank.

International Trade

"Good morning. C.M., can you spare a minute to talk about the plight of Yewkaymia ?"

"Certainly, Simon, carry on."

"Yewkaymia has a minor problem. They cannot produce ships as it's cheaper to buy them from South Korea, so the shipbuilding industry is in trouble."

"They can make clothes. The North of Yewkaymia is crowded by mills."

"Yes, but some of them have been closed down and most of the others converted into mill shops selling goods produced outside Yewkaymia. Clothes can be bought much more cheaply from Thailand or America, so the textile industry has almost disappeared."

"They can still produce coal. Many of their towns were built over coal mines, that's why they suffer so much from subsidence."

"Yes, but they can buy coal cheaper from Australia or South America, so most of their mines have been closed down. The transport of the coal from such great distances produces lots of carbon dioxide, but nobody worries about that."

"They can produce steel."

"There's a European surplus of steel and the American free trade policy doesn't seem to extend to importing steel."

"What about their farming industry?"

"They have got some of the best farmers in the world, but unfortunately some other countries are not quite as fussy about animal welfare or being environmentally friendly as they are. That makes it more difficult for Yewkaymia farmers to be competitive."

"Surely, Yewkaymia has a strong banking and insurance business."

"Yes, but many of those businesses are now owned by foreign companies and many of their banks are using companies in India or China to process their financial transactions, so less people in Yewkaymia are actually employed in banking."

"How will they raise the money to pay for these cheaper products from abroad?"

"They are privatising their public services so that the assets can be bought by foreign companies which brings in money. But they have almost come to the end of that."

"Then what will they do?

"That's a good question, C.M. I hope that someone in their government knows the answer. If that is the problem that Yewkaymia has to face, it must be a hundred times worse for the under-developed countries."

.

Civil rights

Frequently, we hear that doing this, that or the other might impinge on the civil rights of alleged culprits, perhaps 5% of the population. Is there an organisation which sticks up for the civil rights of the innocent 95% of the population, the right to walk the streets or just live in their own homes without the fear of being robbed, injured or killed?

The adoption of the Euro

"Good morning, C.M. The Euro Bureau has reported that for eight minutes between 0215 and 0218 this morning, the U.K. economy passed the five economic criteria. Of course, conditions have changed even since this morning, as they can change at any time, even after we have joined. Some countries in Euroland have already discovered that the Euro bank rate does not suit their trading conditions. Do you still wish to proceed with the plan to sneak in a referendum on the Euro when the attention of the public is diverted onto the Golden Jubilee?"

"Definitely, Clarissa. I expect that 60% of the population will be sincerely celebrating the Jubilee and 30% will just be using it as an excuse for a mammoth binge."

"What about the other 20%, C.M.?"

"Oh, they will be fully occupied in a protest march campaigning for the abolition of the monarchy. If we convince the voters that Euro is a new brand of Lager being offered at BOGOF, we will be home and dry."

Single faith schools or multi-faith schools

Perhaps I should start by saying that, if Church of England and Roman Catholic Schools are given grants towards their upkeep, it is only logical and just that such grants should be available to the schools of other faiths or Christian denominations.

At the same time, I believe that single-faith schools are socially divisive and go against racial harmony and integration. Some single-faith schools also tend to be single culture and single nationality. It may be controversial, but I believe that a few organisations seek isolation and shelter for fear that some of their members might be dissuaded from their present beliefs if they mix with people or children who hold different beliefs. I think that if someone is afraid to discuss their beliefs with someone of a different background, then their beliefs cannot be very strong and well-founded.

I would point in the very opposite direction. I favour, as much as possible, multi-faith schools. This proposal is not without its problems. If possible, Roman Catholic families tend to live in the vicinity of a Roman Catholic Church, Muslims in the vicinity of a Mosque and so on. This means that the 'neighbourhood' school might be predominantly R.C. or Muslim or whatever. But that should not stop multi-faith schools being our target.

Where such schools are possible, I suggest that
(a)   religion should be kept out of academic subjects completely
(b)   first thing every Wednesday morning, every pupil could receive religious education in their own faith under the guidance of someone from their own Church, mosque, synagogue, temple or whatever
(e)   pupils should receive outline religious education in ALL faiths, preferably by a teacher who is neutral or fair-minded, so that they get some grasp of what pupils of other faiths believe.

Racial harmony is much more likely to be promoted if pupils of different cultures are playing together in the same team instead of meeting each other on a football or hockey pitch as adversaries.

Out of school activities are likely to be the greatest source of harmony - the school orchestra or brass band (sorry, no pun intended), school plays, debating societies - any activity in which the different cultures are participating together. It is **sharing** a joke, success, even defeat or adversity that brings people together. Remember the comradeship between the people in the London underground bomb shelters.

Plastic bullets

Someone has recommended that the use of plastic bullets by the police against demonstrators/'demonstrators' should be banned as they are too dangerous. There are demonstrators and 'demonstrators'. I hope that no weapons should be needed against real, peaceful, demonstrators. Against 'demonstrators', perhaps plastic bullets could be replaced by the less dangerous weapons used by the 'demonstrators' themselves, petrol bombs, big chunks of concrete or bottles of acid. Personally, I greatly admire the police who confront petrol bombs with ONLY plastic bullets.

Incidentally, whatever happened to 'The Riot Act' ? I seem to remember that 'The Riot Act' could be read by a magistrate and then the civil authority, the police, could request support from the armed forces. We used to talk about reading the riot act when we meant a strong admonition.

Agriculture

"Good morning, C.M.   One of my constituents, Pharma Jiles, has put forward a proposal for rescuing the farming industry. Farming has been bedeviled by BSE, Foot and mouth disease, Bovine tuberculosis, the low price for milk and the refusal of some of our 'colleagues' in Europe to abide by the decisions of the European experts."

"Farming is a vocation, just as teaching was until someone brought in league tables and payment by results. To farming families, farming is a way of life. Their whole lives are centred on their work much more than someone in a profession. But recently, much of their time and mental energy has had to be focused on paying the bills and making ends meet. Our farmers deserve much better than that."

"Mr. Jiles suggests that all the farms should be state owned, the farmers receiving a salary for the work that they do. At the same time, they would keep their basic independence, just as teachers had in the classroom until .... They would be freed from the financial anxiety of securing subsidies, paying for essential and frequent visits by vets, compensation for destroyed carcasses and so on. They could concentrate on what they are supposed to do and what they are good at, farming."

"Their work would then automatically include taking care of the environment, including the maintenance of public paths, gates and stiles."

"The movement of animals would be planned and kept to the bare minimum. This would minimise the spread of infectious diseases. Farmers have good years and bad years - I seem to recall something about seven years of plenty and seven years of famine. There is also variation each year between products, a bad year for soft fruit might be a good year for Cox's Orange Pippins. If all products were under state ownership, these variations would balance each other out. The state would be in a better position to weather the years of famine than a small-scale farmer."

"Leaving everything to the free market may mean that if farmers think that there is to be a high demand for say sugar beet, they may all pile into sugar beet. That will lead to a surplus of sugar beet on the market, the price will fall and there may be surplus and waste. Farmers will not make much money after all. Of course, it may be possible for farmers to sell their crops before they even plant the seeds, but unplanned agriculture is still dodgy."

"Well, Eustace, you have taken my breath away. I'm afraid that his hare-brained scheme is a non-starter. If we managed to get permission from Brussels, we'd never get permission from Uncle Silas, I mean the Global Trading Association. Why don't you ask Pharma Jiles to let you put it to the next meeting of the Farmers' Association? I'm sure that they would laugh all the way to the bank-ruptcy court!"

Prevention is better than cure

Thankfully, the NHS is beginning to place more emphasis on prevention - healthy living. Unfortunately, when their resources are so stretched, they have to give priority to health problems which already exist. But there are some things that they could do without absorbing either too much medical expertise or money.

Some months ago, as I have angina, I told my G.P. that I was afraid of the approaching winter. He arranged for me to see a cardiologist at the nearest major hospital. I was submitted to various tests, including a treadmill. On either my first or second visit, the cardiologist talked to me about angioplasty, stems, heart bypasses and all sorts of things. Nobody could have been kinder or more knowledgeable.

But the names themselves scared me stiff. I asked him "What can I do to help myself?" He replied "Dark chocolate" and "Red wine". I followed his advice and since then I have been a new man. I feel fitter than I have been for years. I am no longer afraid of winter and I haven't had to be referred to the cardiologist since then. I am more grateful to that cardiologist and the NHS than I would have been if I had undergone many operations.

Age Concern Montgomeryshire has produced a "Healthy Living Check Sheet" intended to try to prevent older people from developing problems. Of course, not every medical problem can be prevented, but, if we eliminated the ones that can be prevented, the NHS would have more resources for the others. Perhaps something on those lines could be distributed to patients free of charge at all health centres. If one visit to a doctor was made unnecessary, that would pay for very many leaflets.

A reduced photocopy of "The Healthy Living Check Sheet" is given on the following two pages, pages 39 and 40. The primary author of "The Healthy Living Check Sheet", Age Concern Montgomeryshire and the author of "GULLIVER'S RAMBLINGS" have all given their permission for pages 39 and 40 to be copied freely.

Healthy Living Check Sheet

Produced by Age Concern Montgomeryshire
(Please complete and give it to your Health Visitor or G.P. when you next consult him/her)

NAME: . . . . **DATE** . . . .

ADDRESS: . . . .

FOOD
Which foods do you eat regularly?   Circle these foods wherever they occur

TYPE OF FOOD	WHAT THEY CONTAIN	WHAT THE VITAMIN OR NUTRIENT DOES
Liver, carrots, dark green & yellow vegetables, fish liver oil, milk, eggs, butter & margarine	Vitamin A	Helps fight infections - keeps cells strong. Good for the skin and for seeing in dim light.
Milk, meat, fish, fruit and vegetables, cereals, eggs, nuts, wheat germ, peanut butter	Vitamin B Complex	Helps the breakdown of carbohydrates, proteins and fats to release energy. Essential for our nerves. Helps production of red blood cells. Good for hair and nails. **Cannot be stored in the body so a daily intake is required**
Fresh or frozen fruit and vegetables. some foods have Vitamin C added.	Vitamin C	Helps fight infection, helps absorb iron (see below). Good for skin. **Cannot be stored in the body so a daily intake is required.**
Liver, fish oil, milk, breakfast cereals, butter and margarine, egg yolks.	Vitamin D	It is formed mainly by the action Fortified of **sunlight** on the skin. Helps absorb and use calcium and phosphorous for strong bones and healthy teeth.
Wheat germ, vegetable oil, whole grain cereal, Nuts, eggs, peas & beans red wine, dark chocolate, green tea	Vitamin E	Acts as an antioxidant in the body

Other antioxidants |
Yoghurt, eggs, leafy vegetables, fish liver oil.	Vitamin K	Helps blood clotting and liver functioning.
Meat, liver, eggs, dark green vegetables, peas, beans, fried fruit, fortified breakfast cereals.	Iron	Needed for the formation of red blood cells which transport oxygen round the body. This gives us energy.
Dark green vegetables, milk, cheese, fish, beans.	Calcium	Needed for strong bones and teeth. **There is constant demand for this so a regular supply is vital.**

39

HEALTH WARNING

SALT
Salt - found in processed meats, salty snacks, cereals, bread, canned/packet soups and vegetables.   You must ensure that you DO NOT eat too much salt.

SMOKING
Do you smoke? . . . . If so how many a day? . . . .
It has been proved that smoking causes narrowing of the arteries of the legs

ALCOHOL
How much alcohol do you drink a day? . . . .
Drinking too much alcohol can lead to damage to the liver. The recommended maximum level for men is 28 units per week and for women 21 units per week.

EXERCISE

How much exercise do you take? Circle all that apply.

Cycle daily   walk upstairs daily   walk to bus stop   walk 1 mile a week

Swim once a week   do aerobics weekly   walk for 20 minutes a day

Play an active sport (eg squash)   Play bowls weekly   Play golf weekly

What is regular exercise? - You don't need to run a marathon. Exercise briskly for 20 minutes 3 times a week and you will soon notice a difference. But start slowly if you are not used to the exercise and if you have a health problem see your Doctor for advice about an exercise routine. Getting off the bus a stop early or using stairs instead of a lift can have a real benefit. Exercise can help you lose weight so for those on a diet is really useful.

MOTIVATION FOR LIFE

You will keep fitter and happier if you are focussed on someone or something other than yourself. For example, caring for a companion or a pet. Could you offer companionship to a neighbour's dog whilst the neighbour is out at work ? Caring for a pet has a therapeutic affect (provided you do not have an allergy to pets) and you could also be doing a good turn for a neighbour.

Have you got a hobby ?   Have you a friend who is connected to the Internet ?

Are you a member of a local club ? What about Line Dancing, Badminton, Table Tennis, Bingo, Word Puzzles, Whist, Dominoes, Mahjong, Practising or Learning Welsh, Learning a Foreign Language, Group walks......................
For details of local clubs, phone Age Concern Montgomeryshire on 01686 623707

Can you do anything to help AGE CONCERN in their efforts to help older people ?
Perhaps you can, but you don't know it! Why not talk to Age Concern Montgomeryshire about it? Telephone 01686 623707

Please phone the same telephone number for information regarding any of the ideas given above.

Another 'bee in my bonnet' is the lack of the full use of computers by G.P.s. Currently, our Medical Centre uses their computer for appointments and to print out prescriptions. I would like to see this use extended to provide WRITTEN information and WRITTEN instructions to be given to patients. For example -

DIAGNOSIS As the result of my examination, you have been diagnosed as having
      (A) CHRONIC LYMPHATIC LEUKAEMIA
      (B) ANGINA

(A)   EXPLANATION
CHRONIC LYMPHATIC LEUKAEMIA is ....

      TREATMENT
XXXXXXXXXXXXXXXXXXXXXX   (I am currently in remission)

      SELF-HELP
FRESH AIR, EXERCISE, HEALTHY DIET

(B)   EXPLANATION
ANGINA is ....

      TREATMENT
ASPIRIN DISPERSIBLE   half tablet daily
                     This is intended to ....
                     Likeliest side-effects ....

IKOREL   one tablet twice a day
                     This is intended to ....
                     Likeliest side-effects ....

ATENOLOL   one tablet each morning
                     This is intended to ....
                     Likeliest side-effects ....

IMDUR   one tablet once a day
                     This is intended to ....
                     Likeliest side-effects ....

GLYCERYL TRINITRATE   as required
                             This is intended for use when angina pain is
                             severe
                             Likeliest side-effects ....

          SELF-HELP : DIET
Dark green vegetables e.g. sprouts, broccoli
Oily fish e.g. salmon
Moderate quantity of RED wine
Moderate quantity of DARK chocolate
          SELF-HELP : EXERCISE
At least 1 mile or 5 km per day
          OTHER SELF-HELP
Adopt a dog or 'Share-a-dog'!

Many G.P.'s do not have sufficient time with each patient to explain fully
either the problem(s) that the patient has or the exact purpose of the various
medications prescribed   or the possibilities for **SELF-HELP**.

If this information were stored on computer,
(a) the time required for a consultation would be minimized
(b) the patient - perhaps elderly - would not be trying to understand and
remember difficult information and instructions when **under stress**
(c) should it be necessary, there would be no doubt about exactly what
the doctor told the patient.

In these days when computer memories are large and there are CD's, this
information could be held in many languages to assist patients whose mother
tongue is not English. It would not then matter so much that the G.P. and
the patient did not have a common language. Perhaps the information could
also be given to a patient in Braille.

Prevention is better than war

I believe that Sir Winston Churchill once said "JAW JAW is better than WAR
WAR." Very few sane people who have actually been involved in a war
want to be involved in another. Within living memory, The League of Nations
was a dismal failure in preventing war. The United Nations has done VERY
much better, but I suggest that it has mostly been trying to restore peace
than to prevent the war or civil war starting.

Once a war has started, it becomes increasingly difficult to stop it and keep the peace. Every death, injury or damaged house gives rise to more and more bitterness. Even a minor dispute can quickly escalate into outright conflict, with no holds barred. We have certainly seen that also within living memory.

Two numbers are much more likely to be different than to be the same. We might say that it is a fluke if they are the same. Similarly, two people or two nations are much more likely to disagree than to agree. There has to be much more effort - and perhaps money - spent **preserving peace** than to **making war**. No, I am not a pacifist. I was one before World War II but the Luftwaffe very soon changed that. But I suggest that every effort should be made to avoid conflict anywhere in the world.

What can be done? Sometime during the 'Cold War', the Soviet Union was desperately short of grain. At the same time, the United States had more than enough grain. Why didn't Uncle Silas use the 'hot line' to Moscow to say "Hello, Ivan, I understand that you're a bit short of grain. We've got a bit to spare. Would you mind if I sent you a couple of million tons free of charge, just as a gesture of goodwill?" When they'd picked him up from the floor, Ivan might have said "Yes, please. Have we got anything of which you are short?"

The United Nations has troops and observers in many parts of the world doing an excellent job keeping possible combatants apart. Could the U.N. have some more observers - spies, if you like - throughout the world just watching for **possible** causes of conflict. Perhaps a yellow signal to say "send out more observers", an amber signal to say "chair a meeting between the two sides" and a red signal to say "send out troops to keep them apart ASAP".

Wouldn't it have been easier to resolve the problems between Israel and Palestine if the U.N. had brokered a deal between Israel and the surrounding Arab nations when the state of Israel was created? Every suicide bomb and every reprisal has made the problem more difficult.

Another problem that has remained unresolved since India and Pakistan became independent is that of Indian-occupied Kashmir. I believe that the fault lies with the people who drew the frontier lines on the map at that crucial time. I have been fortunate enough to visit Indian-occupied Kashmir. It is a truly beautiful place - Srinagar, Dal Lake etc.

I can understand the Indians not wishing to lose it, just as England would not wish to lose the Lake District. But has anyone ever asked the inhabitants of that area what they want? The result might mean a transfer of sovereignty, but surely exchanging some territory occupied by a discontented population together with an unhappy unfriendly neighbour for a happy friendly neighbour would be a win-win bargain. India would also gain much respect and admiration from the rest of the world.

I have the greatest respect for the current Secretary General of the U.N. but the present role of the U.N. makes me think of a football match in which the referee only takes part when the two teams are kicking each other's heads in or a cricket match in which the umpires only take part when the two teams are using the stumps to kill each other!

Why can't disputes be settled by some neutral international court? Even if one side felt that the decision was wrong or unfair, surely a wrong decision is better than a disastrous war. I also include potential civil wars. "No, no outsider must interfere, that would endanger our national sovereignty. We would much rather sacrifice thousands of lives and millions of limbs."

Perhaps negotiators should be locked in a room and told that they weren't going to be allowed out until they had agreed on a settlement. Alternatively, international trade sanctions could be imposed on both sides in the conflict, with no sanction breaking allowed.

There used to be widely accepted rules : in football, "The referee's decision is final ; in cricket "The umpire's decision is final" ; in newspaper competitions "The editor's decision is final". In international matches, the referees are frequently chosen from a neutral country. If those rules apply in important things like sports, they ought to apply in more trivial things like 'war or no war', only involving millions of lives.

In this book, we have mentioned or hinted at three possible conflicts. In each situation, the solution could be obtained easily and quickly by simply asking the inhabitants. We are not talking about two opponents moving plastic pieces on a chess board, manoeuvring to win a game. We are talking about live human beings who have got their own feelings and aspirations. The right to self-determination should be one of the rules of membership - of the Commonwealth, the European Union and then perhaps even the United Nations.

The right to privacy

"Good morning, C.M. I am glad to hear that you have proposed a law to prevent the unauthorised use of DNA samples. It would be dreadful if a husband could know the identity of the father of his wife's baby. It's really got nothing to do with him, has it? It's purely his wife's business. Of course, he might be slightly suspicious if the new baby had brown eyes and big feet whereas their other children had blue eyes and small feet, but that's no reason why he should be allowed to know for certain one way or the other."

Disagreement and evil

There is no question that there is evil in the world. But just because you disagree with someone else, if your beliefs are different from theirs, it does not mean that they are evil. Perhaps you might regard them as intellectually blind - or it might be you, yourself, that is intellectually blind.

Democracy, what democracy?

"Good morning, C.M. Can you spare a few minutes to talk about the electoral system?"

"Come in, Sharmila. Certainly, but I don't know what there is left to talk about. I've rejected proportional representation by the single transferable vote and the crazy idea of electing one third of the members each year, what else is there?"

"Well, C.M., Ms Rosamund Schubert, another of my constituents has suggested that, whether its first past the post or proportional representation, we are still giving the electors the choice of three of more things that they don't want. She suggests that, for real democracy, we should ask the electors just what they do want."

"That sounds a bit radical, Sharmila. Anyway, I don't see how it could work. We can't possibly go round asking every elector what they want. The election would take months, if not years."

"Well, C.M., you might not have experienced it, but, at one time, many of our school examining boards used what they called 'Objective testing' or 'Multiple Choice Questions' as part of their examinations. The examinees indicated their answers by drawing horizontal lines into one of five boxes, depending on their choice of answer. Very successful, it was too."

"The multiple choice answer sheets were marked electronically, extremely quickly, accurately and cheaply. I know one Chief Examiner who even wondered whether they needed to continue with the traditional written papers as the scores produced by the 'Multiple choice questions' were so close to those produced by the traditional papers."

"Sorry, C.M. That is a diversion. Anyway, Rosamund suggests that the same system could be applied to the election. The electors would indicate what policies they want instead of which of three or more candidates, selected by the hierarchy of the party concerned, none of whom might find favour with the electors."

"I think that I follow you, Sharmila. Could you give me some examples of the questions that might be asked?"

"Certainly, C.M. I'll also give you the possible answers."

	A	B	C	D	E
1. Do you think that the railways should be renationalised?	Yes	?	No		
2. Do you think that we should replace the £ by the Euro?	Yes	?	No		
3. Do you think that we should bring back capital punishment?	Yes	?	No		
4. Do you think that Wales should have a Parliament instead of an assembly?	Yes	?	No		
5. Do you think that parcel and mail deliveries should be the monopoly of the Post Office (Royal Mail)?	Yes	?	No		
20. Which party do you support?	Cons	Lib	New Lab		

"Yes, I think I follow you. All the ballot papers would be marked electronically so that we could have all the results in less than an hour, perhaps?"

"Yes, C.M."

"But wouldn't that change the roles of Ministers and M.P.s?"

"Yes, it would. Ministers would be advising and guiding instead of dictating policy. M.P.s would be helping their constituents instead of being division fodder some of the time."

"A leading computer firm is producing a system whereby clubbers in a night club can press one of two buttons to indicate whether or not they like the so-called music being played, for example 'BOOM BOOM BOOM pause' or 'BOOM BOOM pause BOOM'. If the public can have a say in something as important as that, shouldn't the public also have a say in the future of the country?"

"Oh dear, Sharmila, I am certainly not a dictator but some of my ministers are. I'm sorry but it's just a non-starter. Perhaps you need a long holiday, Of course, the Party that calls themselves 'democrat' might introduce the idea to obtain the views of their party members." *(Hint, hint)*

Capital punishment, hospitals and prisons

"Excuse me, C.M., can you spare a few minutes to talk about the death penalty, hospitals and prisons?"

"Of course , Amina, but I don't see the connection between those three."

"I am afraid that the connections are money and personpower. As you know, I am only a 'new girl', so that I need some guidance from you, C.M. I have a lot of questions, but no answers."

"Ask away. Let me have all the questions and then I'll think about the matter and give you my decisions tomorrow."

"Everyone agrees that violence breeds violence. That's why we abolished corporal punishment and the death penalty."

"How many murders were there in 1946 and how many in 2001?"

"Is there less violence now than there was in 1946?"

"Was the abolition of the death penalty just a knee-jerk reaction to the execution of so many innocent people in Europe simply because of their race?"

"How many people in prison are convicted murderers?"

"What percentage is that of the whole prison population?"

"How much money and personpower does it cost to maintain those murderers in prison?"

"How many innocent lives could be saved if those resources were redirected into the hospitals?"

"How many lives could be restored if those resources were redirected into the education, training and rehabilitation of much less serious offenders who now leave prison simply to offend again?"

"Amina, surely no one is advocating the restoration of hanging?"

"No, certainly not, C.M., but some people wonder about a quick painless termination. Of course, the last thing that anyone wants is to execute an innocent man, although some callous people might just call that 'collateral damage'. I prefer to think that the recent advances in detection and the option of a 'not proven' verdict should eliminate that possibility."

"One last question, C.M. Can you explain why it is morally acceptable to 'take out' permanently a soldier whose only 'crimes' were to be born in the wrong country at the wrong time and to be somewhat ignorant of the political geography of the South Atlantic whereas it is not morally acceptable to terminate someone who has enjoyed torturing and then murdering several innocent children or someone who has set fire to a house so as to murder three adults and five children?"

"Well, Amina, the first case was war whereas the second is a purely civilian matter."

"With all due respect, C.M., I wish you would explain that to the elderly people in my constituency. They have known an old lady killed for the sake of her fish-and-chips and an old man killed for trying to prevent a thug from beating his wife. They consider that war, war against evil and crime. They can remember the days when 'good honest crooks' would have done everything they could to help the police to catch the perpetrators of such evil crimes."

"I will try to get the figures you want, Amina, but probably the matter should be left until after the next election. Then the other lot might have to deal with it."

Abortion and Voluntary Euthanasia

Some life organisations lump together abortion and voluntary euthanasia as though they were exactly the same. They both involve the death of a human being, but that is as far as the similarity goes.

I think that, in some exceptional cases such as the result of rape, abortion is regrettable but justified. The love of a mother or 'legal father' towards the result of a rape cannot equal the love of a mother or real father towards a normal baby. In those circumstances, abortion might be in the interest of the baby as well as in the interest of the mother and the 'legal father'. However, abortion just because a birth would be inconvenient is quite different.

Different in the opposite direction is voluntary euthanasia. I don't see what good there is keeping someone, who is in constant pain or agony, perhaps frustrated because they are incapable of doing even the most basic tasks for his/her self, alive against his/her will. What difference is there between that and deliberate torture?

Personally, I am a coward. I don't want to end my life being tortured and I do not believe that a loving God would want that either. Of course, there must be adequate precautions. I once told my wife that I wanted to be cremated, but only after two doctors had signed the death certificate. Probably there should be even greater safeguards before voluntary euthanasia.

School administration

"Good morning, C.M. The Association of School Principals is very concerned about the increasing load to be borne by their members. I've got some suggestions for which I would like your approval."

"Certainly, Lancelot, carry on."

"We would supplement the principal of the school by a bursar to take care of financial matters, a personnel officer to take care of staff recruitment and the ebb and flow of supply staff, a full-time counsellor to take care of the personal problems of both pupils and staff and a full-time solicitor to take care of the increasing number of litigation problems."

"That sounds great, Lancelot, but what would be left for the Principal to do?

"Oh, he would just be involved with the less important task of organising the actual education of the pupils. Of course, to pay for these extra four members of the administrative team, the school would have to lose twenty members of the teaching staff."

"Fine. Target date 31st June 2002. Tell the Heads to fire away!"

Gleaned in the Park

This morning, I picked up the empty box which had contained a replica pistol or automatic called "The jackal in the heather". Relying on my memories of 1940, the replica itself must be both life-size and life-like. The warnings on the empty box were :
"Please retain this for future reference. Not suitable for children under 14 years old." "WARNING : Choking hazard small parts. Not for persons under 14 years." "WARNING * Not suitable for persons under the age of 14 due to the risk of inappropriate firing of the gun at other persons. * Choking hazard small parts, not suitable for children under 14 years. * Do not aim at eyes or face. * Do not use at point blank range. * Do not shoot at humans or animals. * Read carefully the instructions before use. * Recommended for use under adult supervision only."

Next week's news (fictitious) :

"I'm sorry, Mummy, I didn't mean to blind Jane's left eye. I only wanted to 'have a go' after Tom left it on a chair when he went to the loo."

"Why didn't you read the warnings?"

"Mummy, you know that I can't read yet. Anyway, Tom left the box giving the warnings in the park."

Next year's news (fictitious) :

"Judge awards compensation of £250,000 to be paid by the distributor of replica pistols for the loss of the sight in one eye."

The box, which gives the correct name of the product and the address of the distributor, has been retained and will be given to the appropriate authority on request.

Recreational Drugs

The Government is concerned about the misuse of so-called recreational drugs. How much research has there been into why people, mostly youngsters, feel the need to use drugs? Most people go through bad patches. I certainly have, at one time I was suicidal. I never felt the need to take drugs. I think I kept going by throwing myself into my work, all the things that I was doing. My prop was job satisfaction. Is the lack of job satisfaction these days the root of the problem?

The Global Trading Association

I am probably completely wrong, but the impression that I get of the GTA is that it is dominated by the richer, most developed, countries to help them to sell as much as they can to those in the rest of the world who can afford to buy from them. As for the poorest countries with less natural resources, tough!

In my opinion, the organisation of trade should not just depend on who can produce things the cheapest, but also on what countries can produce. I suggest that a benevolent Global Trading Association would
(a) ask each country what they can produce, for example, the West Indies might say "Sugar cane, Rum and cricketers", Brazil might say "Coffee, Corned beef and footballers"
(b) find out how much the world NEEDS of each product
(c) organise worldwide production and distribution on the basis that
  (1) priority in the allocation of the production of a certain product should be given to those countries who cannot produce anything or very little else, whether their product is the cheapest or not
  (2) if possible, every country can produce AND SELL at least three products, to cover the possibility of a failure in the harvest of one product
  (3) the distance between production and consumption should be as little as possible to minimise carbon dioxide emission

If we created a world market in which EVERY country could produce AND SELL SOMETHING, there would be less need for hand-outs which deprive the recipients of their dignity and self-respect. But NO country should restrict food production when people elsewhere in the world are starving.

Sympathy

"Hello, Gull. I am sorry to hear that you have broken your right leg. But you should be thankful, you might have been a horse."

Renewable energy sources

Fossil fuels are a limited resource. Is it also true that taking fossil fuels containing latent heat out of the ground and using them to produce actual heat not only produces carbon dioxide but must also produce global warming?

Wind turbines are a clean source of renewable energy, but many people say "NIMBY (not in MY back yard). We don't want OUR horizon contaminated by tall windmills." When BBC television aerials first appeared on house roofs, many people considered them unsightly. Now no one notices them. The same thing occurred when satellite aerials started to appear. If EVERY house had a **solar panel** on its roof, how much power could be saved in the whole country? If the government lent customers the cost of the panel and installation repayable over the 'break-even' time at zero interest, even 'old codgers' like myself would go for it.

Most street lamps are erected on standards in the shape of an inverted **L**. If the top of every lamp-standard was covered by a horizontal solar panel, how much power would that save?

My car does about **six** miles per day and sits outside in the sun for at least six hours. If necessary, it could be left outside for much longer. How much petrol could be saved if the roof of the car carried a solar panel?

O.K., solar panels are expensive at present. So were calculators not many years ago. I remember paying £120 for an electro-mechanical calculator which would add, subtract, multiply and divide - nothing else. Perhaps two years later, I paid £120 for an electronic calculator which would add, subtract, multiply, divide and take a square root - nothing else. For the last few years, you have been able to buy an electronic calculator for less than £10 which will carry out more operations than I could list in many pages of this book.

If the government took solar panels seriously, the cost could be reduced considerably and very quickly.

Truancy and the school curriculum

"Good afternoon, C.M. You remember that you asked me to try to find out why the problem of truancy is getting worse and worse. I haven't been able to obtain any concrete evidence, but a few ideas have been given to me."

"Carry on, Charlotte, They must be better than nothing."

"First, the most common word used by youngsters is "BORING!". The reasons why they may be bored in school are (a) they are brought up with fast-moving films on television or perhaps even faster computer games, so anything in the classroom is slow by comparison (b) sometimes the curriculum that they are forced to follow is unsuitable for their ability or inclination."

"Before 'comprehensives' were brought in, pupils in the despised secondary modern schools could be very happy, thank you very much, learning carpentry, metalwork, typing, dressmaking, cookery and so on. They were being taught things at which they could SUCCEED and that they KNEW had relevance to REAL life."

"We are bringing in specialist schools for music geniuses, and so on, but what about specialist schools for the electricians, builders, plumbers, motor mechanics and so on that we desperately need. These days, with C.D.s, we only need a handful of brilliant musicians, but we need thousands of artisans - if anybody still knows what that word means. Part of the trouble is that education is led by academics, many of whom think that the only skills of consequence are academic skills. There should be more respect for the practical skills."

"Second, part of the trouble may be the absence of someone at home, when in most households, both husband and wife (or their equivalent) are out at work. Obviously, I am certainly not going to advocate that intelligent females, who are now surpassing boys in school, should once again be tied to the kitchen sink."

"But I wonder if we should introduce a six day working week in which the husband spends three days at work and three at home and wife does the same, sharing child care and domestic work between them. Of course, special arrangements might have to be made for Parliament."

"On a slightly different topic, one ex-teacher suggested that the present examining system is flawed. She suggests that school exams should be on the same lines as Royal School of Music exams in which pupils enter for an exam at a certain grade when they are ready for that grade. With adequate staff levels and 'setting' within school years, there might be pupils in year 8 doing grade 7 Maths, grade 8 Maths and grade 9 Maths."

"Using that system, when pupils move from one school to another, the pupil would simply tell the Head of Maths what grade he/she had attained in order to be put into the right set."

"Well, Charlotte, you have certainly given me enough food for thought, if not for indigestion. I'll have to come back to you on it later."

Government finance

Rightly or wrongly, I have gained the impression that Government accounts ignore the difference between Fixed Assets and Current Assets, if they consider Fixed Assets at all. If a business man sold a computer which was 'on his books' at £250 for £250, that would produce no income. If he sold the same computer for £200, that would produce a loss or expenditure of £50.

I only suspect that, when the government privatises something, they treat the proceeds as income so that they can use the proceeds to balance against expenditure and reduce income tax. But that means that, if they wanted to renationalise the something, there is no money in the kitty to allow them to do it.

Surplus computers

The firm, for which a friend of mine works, disposed of two unwanted computers (slower than the ones that they currently use) by giving them to two school children who did not have a computer of any type for use at home.

They wish to encourage some organisation - perhaps a Rotary Club or Chamber of Trade - to take up the idea by encouraging their members to hand in their redundant computers for checking over and distribution to children who could make good use of them. Other outlets would be senior citizens in this country or some organisation who could despatch them for use in developing countries.

Respect and Pay

"Good morning, C.M. You wanted us to get together to produce some guidelines regarding pay settlements so as to avoid leap-frogging. You may remember that, two years ago, you set up a market research agency called Asker Scilly. Well, they have just produced their first report, about three pages long. They organised an internet e-mail survey to establish a league table of the respect that the public had for different occupations. Of course, I don't know how truly representative it is. I voted nearly two hundred times myself."

"Great, Rosemary, that sounds marvellous. I'm all for league tables. What were the results?"

"The most respected were
1.   Doctors, surgeons and veterinary surgeons
2.   Nurses and veterinary nurses
3.   Teachers
4.   Para-medics and firefighters"
The least respected were
1.   Lottery jackpot winners
2.   Heavyweight boxers
3.   Popstars
4.   Premier Footballers
5.   Managing Directors
6.   M.P.s"

"Fine, Rosemary. That gives us a start. I suggest

Lottery jackpot winners	£5,000,000 for two minutes
Heavyweight boxers	£8,000,000 for one evening
Pop stars	£4,000,000 for one disc
Premier footballers	£50,000 per week
Managing Directors	£400.000 per year plus an annual bonus of £300,000 if successful and a golden handshake of £2,000,000 if the company goes bust
M.P.s	State secret
Para-medica and firefighters	£27,000 per year
Teachers	£26,000 per year
Nurses and veterinary nurses	£25,000 per year
Doctors and veterinaries	£24,000 per year"
Surgeons to repair boxers	£23,000 per year"

"But, C.M., that means that the more respected people are, the less they will get paid."

"I know, Rosemary, that's just what would make it fair. People shouldn't expect to have everything, both respect and lots of money."

"But, C.M., that's just what we expect."

"I'm sorry, Rosemary, we'll have to leave it at that. I've got another appointment."

Last minute snippet

A householder, who has been burgled frequently, has been given permission to protect his home with razor wire provided that he erects a warning notice outside his house.

Seen outside a neighbouring house :

WARNING TO BURGLARS

The left-hand rear hob of the electric cooker in the kitchen might still be very hot. Please be careful.

Stop press

"Good morning, C.M. Have you heard about the very generous annual bonus paid to Ms Obese Feline, the boss of By2much ? Don't you think that it is OTT when we are trying to encourage wage restraint? It's more than the GNP of some Third World countries. It would take a teacher more than ten years hard work to earn that much."

"Yes, but there is no comparison between the two, Donald. Ms Obese Feline is earning MONEY whereas school teachers are only helping to produce mature educated PEOPLE. Anyway, I've never heard of a single teacher making a unanimous donation of £ 200,000 to party funds."

GULL IVER'S closing remarks

(a) "You know, Gull, I'm beginning to think that you haven't got 100% confidence in the powers that be."

"You're very perceptive, Gerald. I think 99% perhaps, but 100% definitely no."

(b) I am pleased to note that, during the last few days of my ramblings, many well-respected people are singing my songs. I am truly delighted, but also thankful that my ramblings will be released as a medley or album and not as a single.

(c) The motto of a brilliant man is "If you know enough to ask the question, you are halfway to the answer." I hope that my ramblings will at least give you some questions.

(d) As they say in the very centre of civilisation **"If't cap fits, wear it."**

(e) I should like to record my very insincere thanks to Alick Hartley for so unfaithfully recording my ramblings to the best of his unfortunately very limited ability.

Publisher's note

Any requests for help in understanding Gull Iver's subtler points should not be addressed to the publishers as we cannot understand them either. Gull Iver himself can be reached in Outer Bongolia by telephone, each weekday between 2455 and 2510. The call charges are £543.21 per minute and his telephone number is Outer Bongolia

∧ ∪ ∨ ⊕   ∇⊃⟨◇   ∨ ∨ ∇ ∧   ⊤ □ Å ∩

To avoid mistakes, we will repeat that number.

∧ ∪ ∨ ⊕   ∇⊃⟨◇   ∨ ∨ ∇ ∧   ⊤ □ Å ∩

Author's apologies

The author wishes to express his sincere apologies

(a) for the extreme opinions of GULL IVER. He has just not been able to keep pace with the rapid moral changes that have taken place since the public spirited attitude of most people during World War II. He has become all bitter and twisted.

(b) to the several political parties who have not been mentioned in this book.

(c) for any items which have past their 'sell-by dates' by the time that you read this book.

(d) for forgetting to ask the printer to print the text of the book on nonflammable paper.

(e) for all the items that were not included in this book because Gull was not so inspired in time. Writing this book was like trying to hit a moving target. (I hope that a member of the hoi polloi is permitted to use that word.) The shutters had to be brought down at some point and I chose 0900 on the 24 May 2002.

(f) to anyone who feels that he/she has been punched above the belt.

(g) to people in Scotland, Wales and Northern Ireland who consider that the book is England biased. My excuse is that I prefer to write about things about which I know very little rather than about things about which I know nothing.

Author's acknowledgements of thanks (1)

The author wishes to offer his insincere thanks

(a) to several political parties for the many gifts which he has received as a reward for not mentioning them in this book.

(b) to the ENGEXAM public examinations board for prescribing "GULL IVER'S RAMBLINGS" as an ENGLISH set book for the June 2002 examinations - pity that it wasn't June 2003 so that copies would have been available for the candidates to study the book.

(c) to many leading publishers for their offers of advance royalties varying between £0.07 and £0.15 for the publishing rights to the book.

(d) to the C.M. for his very generous gift of a one-way ticket to Patagonia together with a Swedish-English Dictionary for use on arrival.

End of non-government sanity warning

The non-government sanity warning does not apply to the remaining pages in this book. All the information is genuine and, we hope, correct.

Author's acknowledgements of thanks (2)

The author wishes to offer his sincere thanks

(a) to Dr. John Harries, Newtown Medical Practice and the Royal Shrewsbury Hospital. They were all awarded A*

(b) for the divine provision of three wonderful dogs - "Sally", "Heather" and "Lady".

(c) to Hafren Vets, Newtown, for their loving care and support, not only of his three dogs, but also of their elderly owner. They were also awarded A*

(d) to his three faithful dogs for keeping him healthy, if very far from wealthy and wise.

(e) to Jonathan Swift, author of Gulliver's Travels. Any resemblance between this book and Gulliver's Travels is virtually impossible.

(f) to BBC Radio 4/World Service for the seeds from which most of the monkey puzzles have grown. I have very much enjoyed writing this book, even if nobody reads it. **Thank you very much, BBC Radio 4/World Service.**

(g) to Howys Ltd, Newtown, Powys for maintaining the computer without which this book could not have been produced.

(h) to The Export Association, Welshpool for assistance with translation.

(i) to Kim Selene Davies for the illustration on page 59.

(j) to John Savill and Ken Davies for their helpful suggestions and their kind offer of the use of a bonfire.

(k) to Sally Harvey, Newtown, Powys for her invaluable legal advice in connection with the contents of this book.

(l) to Robert Edwards of St. Idloes Press for producing a top quality book.

AUTHOR'S NOTES

(1) For all its faults, I am still thankful that I live in Britain.

(2) Even at this late stage, the author would welcome serious proposals from big publishers for taking over the publication of this book and any subsequent books. A suitable arrangement could be made with IMPART BOOKS.

End of non-government sanity warning

The non-government sanity warning does not apply to the remaining pages in this book. All the information is genuine and, we hope, correct.

The next few pages give details of other books published or distributed by IMPART BOOKS. Details of even more books are given in our web site

www.books.mid-wales.net

"THE TALE OF THREE DOGS" 1-874155-13-5

This book, written by Alick Hartley, is the true story of how three dogs gave new life to a lonely old widower. It is most enjoyable to read and is well illustrated. It would be especially of interest to all dog lovers.
88 pages · Paperback · Perfect binding · 57 black-and-white illustrations

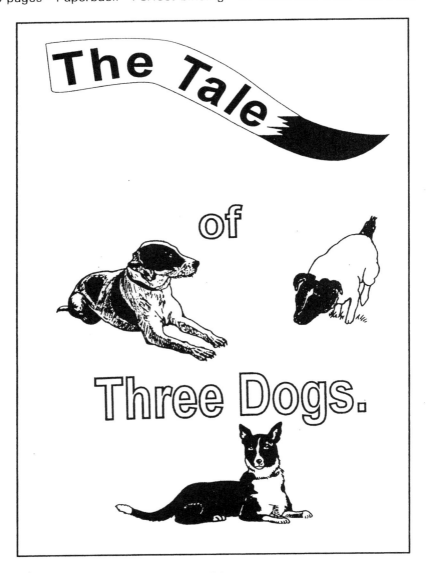

"ENGLISH LANGUAGE PICTURE CROSSWORDS" 1-874155-39-9

This 60 page A4 book contains 50 crosswords in the English language, each clue being a specially drawn black-and-white picture. This book is intended to help people to remember basic English vocabulary. It would be particularly useful for children and adults whose mother tongue is not English.

A Picture Word Book in **FOUR** languages - English, French, Arabic and German. **1122** specially drawn , easy to recognise, black-and-white illustrations, arranged under 46 topics. Each illustration is accompanied by the appropriate English word and the equivalent word in French, Arabic and German. 226 pages - 14.5 cm by 15 cm - Paperback - perfect binding.

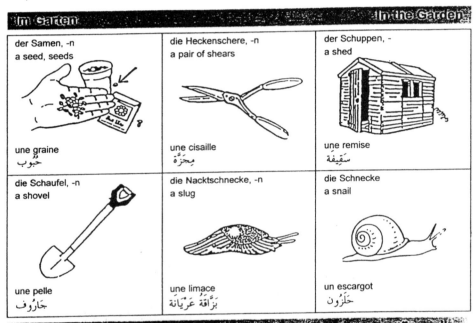

Im Garten   In the Garden

der Samen, -n a seed, seeds	die Heckenschere, -n a pair of shears	der Schuppen, - a shed
une graine حَبُوب	une cisaille مِجَزَّة	une remise سَقِيفة
die Schaufel, -n a shovel	die Nacktschnecke, -n a slug	die Schnecke a snail
une pelle جَارُوف	une limace بَزَّاقَة عَرْيَانة	un escargot حَلَزُون

Au Jardin

"STEP-BY-STEP GUIDE FOR THE HONORARY TREASURER" 0-9513233-1-8

This book, by Alick Hartley, provides easy-to-follow guidance on the keeping of simple manual double-entry accounts as may be necessary for a small sports club or similar activity. General introduction, The Cash book, Cash transactions, Money paid direct to the club's bank accounts, Money paid out by cheque, Withdrawals from the current account by direct debit or standing order, Totalling the cash book and bank reconciliation, The ledger, Posting receipts to the ledger, Posting payments to the ledger, The trial balance, The Income and Expenditure account and the Balance Sheet, The year end procedure, Auditing the club accounts, Petty cash imprest system.
48 pages - 20.9 cm by 14.3 cm - Paperback - Stapled cover.

"THE KEY TO WALES" 1-874155-33-X

"THE KEY TO WALES" is intended as a tribute to the nation which has turned the key, opened the door and welcomed the author, B. Trevor Rogers, and his family, allowing them to share their friendship and hospitality.

It is hoped that the book will encourage understanding between the Welsh people and the people in the rest of Britain, dispelling many of the hitherto unanswered questions in the minds of those living outside the principality.

Why is there any need for Wales to be identified as a separate nation?
From where did the Welsh people originate?
Why are they so possessive about the Welsh language?

62 pages - 21 cm by 15 cm - Paperback - Perfect binding - 24 illustrations.

"STATISTICS BOOK ONE" 81-202-0308-9

This book, by Alick Hartley, B.Sc., covers Pictorial Representation, Measures of average or location, Measures of dispersion or spread, The linear transformation of data, The elementary analysis of time series, Weighted means, Scatter diagrams, Probability, Approximations and errors, Sampling and questionnaires, Spearman's rank correlation coefficient, Revision questions.
288 pages - A5 - Paperback - Perfect binding.
This book has also been published in ROMANIAN and will shortly be published in RUSSIAN.

"STATISTICS BOOK TWO"   81-202-0524-3

This book, by Alick Hartley, B.Sc., follows on from BOOK ONE. It covers The use of random numbers for sampling, Probability, Scatter diagrams, Spearman's rank correlation coefficient, Permutations and combinations, The Binomial Distribution, The Poisson Distribution, The Normal Distribution, The mean and standard deviation of the means of samples, Comparing the means of two large samples, The fitting of a distribution of a given type to observed data.
252 pages - A5 - Paperback - Perfect binding.

"SIMPLIFIED ACCOUNTS FOR THE CHARITY TREASURE"   0-9513233-2-6

This book, by Alick Hartley, provides easy-to-follow guidance on the keeping of simple manual double-entry accounts as may be necessary for a small charity or a small branch of a nationwide charity. General introduction, The Cash book, Cash transactions, Money paid direct to the charity's bank accounts, Money paid out by cheque, Withdrawals from the current account by direct debit or standing order, Totalling the cash book and bank reconciliation, The ledger, Posting receipts to the ledger, Posting payments to the ledger, The trial balance, The Income and Expenditure account and the Balance Sheet, The year end procedure, Auditing the charity accounts, Petty cash imprest system.
48 pages - 20.9 cm by 14.3 cm - Paperback - Stapled cover.

"LEARNERS PICTURE WORDBOOK : ENGLISH-RUSSIAN"   985-6092-39-6

This book contains 1200 specially drawn, easy to recognise, black-and-white illustrations, arranged under 49 topics. Each illustration is accompanied by the appropriate English word, the international phonetic symbols giving the pronunciation of the English word, the equivalent Russian word and the international phonetic symbols giving the pronunciation of the Russian word. The English words are classified - adjective, adverb, noun, proposition, verb.
128 pages - 25.8 cm by 16.5 cm - Paperback - Perfect binding.

"LEARNERS PICTURE WORDBOOK : ENGLISH & PHONETICS"
81-7181-569-3

This book contains 1200 specially drawn, easy-to-recognise, black-and-white illustrations, arranged under 49 topics. Each illustration is accompanied by the appropriate English word and the International Phonetic symbols giving the pronunciation of each word. The words are classified - adjective, adverb, noun, preposition, verb.
120 pages - 28 cm by 21.5 cm - Paperback - Perfect binding.

alligator (n)	anteater (n)	antelope (n)
'ælɪ,geɪtə	'ænt,iːtə	'æntɪ,ləʊp
ape (n)	baboon (n)	badger (n)
eɪp	bə'buːn	'bædʒə
bat (n)	bear (n)	beaver (n)
bæt	bɛə	'biːvə
bison (n)	buffalo (n)	camel (n)
'baɪs'n	'bʌfə,ləʊ	'kæməl

This 124 page A4 book contains 100 wordsearches in the ENGLISH language and in the WELSH language. Each word is identifiewd by a specially drawn black-and-white picture.

CHWILOTEIRIAU
LLUN
CYMRAEG a
SAESNEG

CLODDIO

DIG

BWYTA

EAT

NEIDIO

JUMP

```
U   N    A   C   Ï   D   U   G   O
E   C   DD   M   I   C   A   I   I
O    I    D   I   E   N   T   F   TH
RH  TH    S   R   Y   C   Y   G   W
H    E   DD   T   N   L   W   O   G
LL   E    D   E   E   O   B   L   W
D    D    A   E   S   DD  F  CH   N
F    Ï    T   F   G   I   N   I   Ï
CH   W    I   F   I   O   N   W   O


P   U   T   D   I   R   P
E   H   I   I   V   K   W
W   S   S   G   J   N   A
E   A   T   U   N   M   V
S   W   M   P   P   I   E
Q   P   K   L   A   W   S
B   C   N   U   R   S   V
```

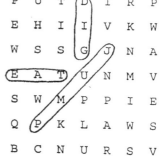

WELSH &
ENGLISH
PICTURE
WORDSEARCHES

"WELSH PICTURE CROSSWORDS"   1-874155-35-6

This 114 page A4 book contains 50 crosswords in the WELSH language, each clue being a specially drawn black-and-white picture.

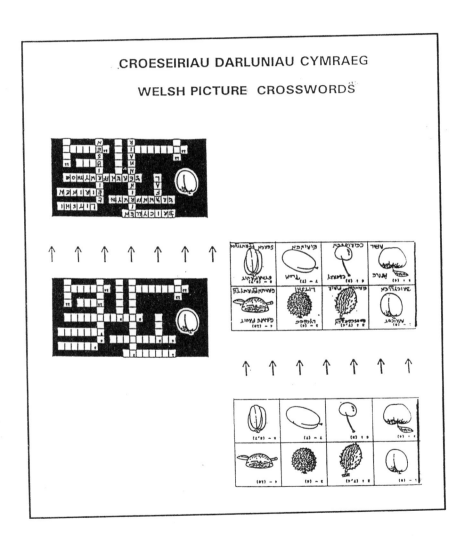

CROESEIRIAU DARLUNIAU CYMRAEG

WELSH PICTURE CROSSWORDS

The non-government sanity warning does not apply to the remaining pages in this book. All the information is genuine and, we hope, correct.

The next few pages give details of "VISUAL CLASSROOM TESTING"

The pages are reduced photocopies taken from the pages of the book "INTRODUCTION TO VISUAL CLASSROOM TESTING" 1-874155-41-0. Should the size of the type of those pages be too small for you to read, the text of "INTRODUCTION TO VISUAL CLASSROOM TESTING" is given in colour in our web site www.books.mid-wales. net from where the text may be downloaded and printed *completely free of charge.*

The whole or part of the contents of "INTRODUCTION TO VISUAL CLASSROOM TESTING" may be printed or copied by any method, either for use or for sale, provided that each book or extract contains the acknowledgement
"Copyright © 2000 IMPART BOOKS, U.K. Used by permission"

Similarly, the whole or part of the book may be translated and published in other languages without further permission provided that each book or extract contains the acknowledgement
"Copyright © 2000 IMPART BOOKS, U.K. Used by permission"

What is VCT ?

Visual Classroom Testing (VCT) is a system whereby a teacher can obtain immediate responses to a question, from every pupil in the class. VCT **complements** the traditional method of teaching, it does not replace it. The use of VCT need not affect the syllabus covered or the order of teaching.

Why do we need VCT ?

The traditional method of teaching is that the teacher teaches a topic or process and then attempts to test the class by stating a question and then asking an individual pupil to give the answer. Teachers are recommended to pause after stating the question - to allow time for the whole class to think out the answer - and then give the name of the particular pupil required to answer.

With an active responsive class, all the pupils may think out what they believe to be the correct answer. However, with a less responsive class, the pupils may not bother to think out the answer until some poor unfortunate pupil's name is given ! Using VCT, every pupil in the class is required to answer, simultaneously.

Even with a responsive class, using the traditional method of teaching, the teacher will probably only have time to extract answers from very few pupils. The teacher will then make his/her judgement on the success of the lesson based on the response of those very few pupils. The teacher may deduce that all is well when in reality the majority of the class may not have understood the lesson taught.

Using VCT, the teacher obtains an answer, correct or incorrect, from **every** pupil in the class. The first time that VCT was used, the teacher was quite dismayed by what he discovered. Almost half the class were quite 'in the dark' about the topic that he thought he had taught satisfactorily. However, some time later, having taught the topic again, this time in simpler words and at a slower speed, he was delighted to find that every pupil in the class had grasped the topic taught. VCT does not permit any false illusions regarding the success or failure of a lesson.

73

How does VCT work ?

Each member of the class is equipped with an answering device such as a cube, a hexagon or an equilateral triangle. When a question is asked, each pupil holds up his/her answering device, displaying his/her answer to the teacher. The teacher is then able to see which pupils have the correct answer and which need help. This can be followed by asking individual pupils how they arrived at their answer.

What equipment is needed by the pupils ?

Each member of the class needs an answering device - (a) a cube (b) a hexagon or (c) an equilateral triangle (using both sides).

(a) a CUBE
a wooden or plastic cube - similar to some toy bricks used by children - the six faces of the cube being clearly labelled A, B, C, D, E and ? respectively as illustrated below. If possible, the faces of the cube should be colour-coded :

     a black letter **A** on a **red** background
     a black letter **B** on an **orange** background
     a black letter **C** on a **yellow** background
     a black letter **D** on a **green** background
     a black letter **E** on a **blue** background
     a black symbol **?** on a **violet** background
as illustrated below.

Countries which do not use the letters A B C D E and ? might simply use the colours red, orange, yellow, green, blue and violet or else use those own symbols instead of A B C D E and ?

Such lettered cubes can be made by simply fastening the net of a cube to the faces of a wooden or plastic cube. The net of a cube is illustrated below :

·OR (b) a HEXAGON,
a rigid hexagon (perhaps cardboard), the six sectors of which are clearly labelled A, B, C, D. E and
? as illustrated below. If possible, the sectors of the hexagon should be colour-coded in the same
way as the cube.

OR (c) an EQUILATERAL TRIANGLE,
an equilateral triangle, the angles on one side of the triangle being clearly labelled A, B and C, the
angles on the other side of the triangle being clearly labelled D, E and ? If possible, the angles of
the equilateral triangle should be colour-coded in the same way as the cube and the hexagon.

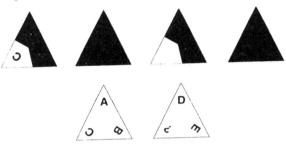

How are the questions presented ?

Each question is asked in the traditional way, but additionally, the class is given a number of
possible answers, usually five. The pupils are also instructed not to attempt to answer until they
are told to do so.

The method by which the question and the possible answers are given to the class will vary very
considerably depending on the equipment - if any - available to the teacher. Possible methods are

(a)   simply reading out the question, allowing time for the pupils to think out their answer, and
       then reading out the possible answers (A) (B) (C) (D) and (E).

(b)   writing or drawing the question on the blackboard and later reading out the possible
       answers.

(c)   presenting the question and possible answers on a LARGE sheet of paper, prepared before
       the lesson.

(d)   supplying each pupil with a printed sheet which gives the question and the possible
       answers.

(e)   the use of an overhead projector.

Can you give me an easy example ?

Question asked   What is the capital city of India ?

Possible answers offered   A   Beijing
                                B   Karachi
                                C   London
                                D   New Delhi
                                E   Washington

The class will then be asked to give their answers.

If a pupil thinks that the correct answer is Beijing, he/she should display the letter A (red)

If a pupil thinks that the correct answer is Karachi, he/she should display the letter B (orange)

If a pupil thinks that the correct answer is London, he/she should display the letter C (yellow)

If a pupil thinks that the correct answer is New Delhi, he/she should display the letter D (green)

If a pupil thinks that the correct answer is Washington, he/she should display the letter E (blue)

If a pupil thinks that none of the answers offered is correct or if the pupil has no idea what the correct answer is, he/she should display the symbol ? (violet).

The teacher can then see how many in the class have got the right answer, how many have got an incorrect answer and how many are in need of help.

What about pupils copying answers ?

At some convenient time, the class should be told that the VCT is **NOT** an examination so that a pupil will gain nothing by cheating, indeed the very opposite. The VCT is intended to help the teacher to help those pupils who need help. Nevertheless, it is possible that a pupil may either copy someone else's answer or simply guess what the answer is. This can be discouraged by asking a particular pupil - who has either the correct answer or an incorrect answer - how he/she obtained his/her answer. For example, "John, how did you get that answer ?" or "Mary, why do you think that the answer is XXXXX ?"   (*Please forgive the use of English names.*)

How effective is the system ?

Giving five possible answers in addition to the question obviously takes more time than just giving the question. Using VCT, the teacher will not have time to ask as many questions as otherwise. However, each question asked will be 20, 30 or 40 times more powerful and effective - depending on the number of pupils in the class. So the use of VCT is actually much more efficient.

76

What about colour-blindness ?

A significant proportion of people - both teachers and pupils - are colour-blind. If this causes difficulty, answering devices should not rely on colour alone. They should have colour AND a symbol, such as A B C D E ? or some other symbols appropriate to the country concerned, for example ● ■ ▲ ✳ ✿ or local flowers. On the other hand, VCT might be of value in the teaching of pupils with hearing or speech difficulties.

When was VCT developed ?

The idea for Visual Classroom Testing (VCT) was given to Alick Hartley, B.Sc. in 1969 and VCT was developed during the succeeding years. Visual classroom tests were published on a small scale in 1987 and 1991. Since then, the system has been improved very considerably. At the same time, IMPART BOOKS have established themselves as producers of educational books for printing and publication world-wide.

How much does it cost to try out and adopt VCT ?

For trying out the system, we will charge you **NOTHING**. Most of the information given in this book is also given in the internet web site **www.bookideas.mid-wales.net** and can be freely downloaded.

For using the sample tests given on pages 9 to 20 of this book, we will charge you **NOTHING**.

For adopting the system, using tests produced by yourself, we will charge you **NOTHING**.

Which tests can we use free of charge, to try the system ?

Page 9	Picture	to	English word
Page 10	Picture	to	word in another language
Page 11	English word	to	Picture
Page 12	Word in another language	to	Picture
Page 13	Arithmetic : Addition of numbers less than 10		
Page 14	Correct spelling of English words - by translation		
Page 15	Correct spelling of English words - from pictures		
Page 16	Correct spelling of English words - stand alone		
Page 17	Plurals of English words		
Page 18	Recognising a country from a map		
Page 19	Finding the capital city of a country		
Page 20	Finding the country given its capital city		

What are the drawbacks or disadvantages of VCT ?

By far the most time-consuming and expensive part of the system is the production of the sets of questions and possible answers. You might try to produce one set of 20 questions and possible answers yourself, to see how much time and effort it requires.

Can you give any guidance regarding producing tests ?

(1)   Generally, there should be roughly an equal number of correct answers A, B, C, D, E.

(2)   There should be only **one** correct answer. For example, there should **not** be answers
(i) "six" and "half a dozen"   or   (ii) 1/2 and 0.5

(3)   If possible. the incorrect answers offered should be 'near misses' , the common mistakes made by 'average' pupils.

(4)   In Mathematics tests, it is helpful to include some questions where the correct answer is NOT one of the possible answers offered. Pupils should respond to this by ? which also means 'the correct answer has not been offered'.

Can IMPART BOOKS offer any ready-made sets of VCT questions ?

IMPART BOOKS have produced a few books containing sets of questions which can be used as they are supplied or after modification to suit the local culture and conditions or after translation into another language.   These books will be supplied to you as cheaply as possible to cover the cost of production and postage/delivery.

The following sets of VCT questions are available either now (21 August 2000) or very soon
(a)   VISUAL CLASSROOM TESTING **Picture to English Book One**
       This book contains 50 pages of 12 questions, similar to the specimen page given on
       page 9 of this book.   ISBN 1 874155 42 9
(b)   VISUAL CLASSROOM TESTING **Picture to English Book Two**
       This book contains 50 pages of 12 questions, similar to the specimen page given on
       page 10 of this book.   ISBN 1 874155 43 7
(c)   VISUAL CLASSROOM TESTING **English to Picture Book One**
       This book contains 50 pages of 12 questions, similar to the specimen page given on
       page 11 of this book.   ISBN 1 874155 44 5
(d)   VISUAL CLASSROOM TESTING **English to Picture Book Two**
       This book contains 50 pages of 12 questions, similar to the specimen page given on
       page 12 of this book.   ISBN 1 874155 45 3
(e)   VISUAL CLASSROOM TESTING **Arithmetic Book One**
       This book contains 50 pages, each page containing up to 20 questions, the format similar
       to the specimen page given on page 13 of this book.   ISBN 1 874155 46 1
(f)   VISUAL CLASSROOM TESTING **Arithmetic Book Two**
       This book contains 50 pages, each page containing up to 20 questions, the format similar
       to the specimen page given on page 13 of this book.   ISBN 1 874155 47 X

The decision is yours

The VCT system has proved to be successful in a number of schools, but we cannot guarantee that it would be successful in your school or in your country. Please try the system for yourself - a trial would cost very little time or money. If the system works for you, the benefit could be tremendous.

		A	B	C	D	E
1		fishing boat	lifebuoy	life jacket	lobster pot	mast
2		oil rig	porthole	sailing boat	lifebuoy	ship
3		starfish	submarine	fishing boat	sea	life jacket
4		lobster pot	mast	oil rig	porthole	sailing boat
5		mast	sea	starfish	submarine	fishing boat
6		life jacket	lobster pot	ship	oil rig	lifebuoy
7		porthole	fishing boat	sea	ship	starfish
8		submarine	sailing boat	lifebuoy	lobster pot	life jacket
9		oil rig	mast	porthole	sailing boat	sea
10		ship	oil rig	submarine	fishing boat	lifebuoy
11		life jacket	lobster pot	mast	starfish	porthole
12		sailing boat	sea	submarine	ship	starfish

79

		A	B	C	D	E
1		gazelle	kangaroo	monkey	otter	panda
2		浣 熊	臭 鼬	蛇	松 鼠	袋 鼠
3		lǎo hǔ	hóu zi	bān mǎ	dèng líng	shuǐ tǎ
4		зилра	черепаха	енот	скунс	змея
5		(سِنْجاب (سَناجِيب)	نَمِر (نُمُر)	سُلَحْفاةُ الْمَاء	بَنْدَة	غَزَالَة (غِزْلان)
6		un kangourou	un singe	une loutre	un panda	un raton laveur
7		das Stinktier	der Tiger	das Eichhörnchen	der Waschbär die Wasserschildkröte	
8		pundamilia	nyoka	nyegere uvundo	paa	kangaruu
9		maimuţă	panda	tigru	veveriţă	şarpe
10		tigre	nutria	tortuga marina	cebra	gacela
11		cangaru	macaco	zebra	panda	tartaruga
12		racŵn	drewgi	sebra	neidr	gwiwer

80

		A	B	C	D	E
1	factory					
2	garage					
3	hotel					
4	hut					
5	lighthouse					
6	prison					
7	market					
8	mosque					
9	church					
10	temple					
11	tower					
12	windmill					

81

	A	B	C	D	E
1 factory					
2 仓 库					
3 fàn diàn					
4 хижина					
5 (مَنَائِر) مَنَارَة					
6 une prison					
7 der Markt					
8 moschee					
9 iglesia					
10 templo					
11 mnara					
12 melin wynt					

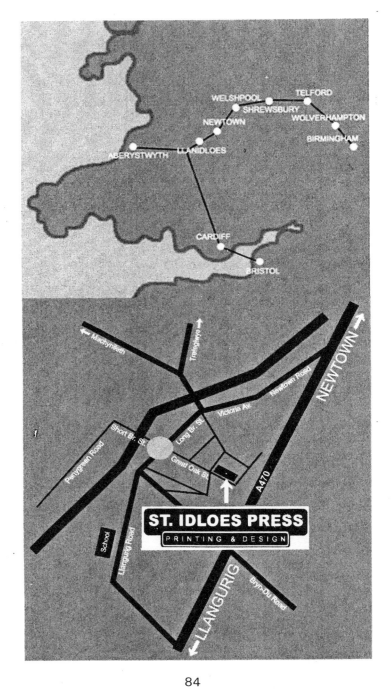